The Cats Who Ran Away

For Sue —
Not simply kin — —
but a dear friend
as well!

Frank

The Cats Who Ran Away

Frank Paine

iUniverse, Inc.

New York Lincoln Shanghai

The Cats Who Ran Away

iUniverse, Inc.

For information address:
iUniverse, Inc.
2021 Pine Lake Road, Suite 100
Lincoln, NE 68512
www.iuniverse.com

Illustrations by the author

ISBN: 0-595-29217-8

Printed in the United States of America

Contents

1

Three To Get Ready

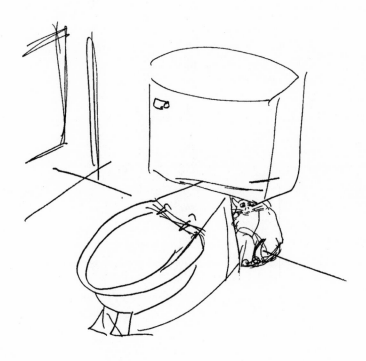

Now don't get me wrong. I like cats.

What faced me though was a problem which might tax my affection for the creatures.

You see, my companion Barbara and I had decided to leave our home in Illinois and move west. That was the easy part. The problem was Barbara's cat Felix. Would he even tolerate travel? Cats, especially older ones, are notorious for their loathing of being bounced around in motor vehicles.

Also, would Felix tolerate me? Ever since I'd known Barbara, the cat had sought other places to be whenever I was around. I think some man had given Felix a hard time in the past.

Could we, two adults traveling in a micro-mini motor home, find happiness sharing our confinement with a large, adult, outdoor, twelve-pound, nine-year old, strong, active—cat? I did not think so.

But as I said, I like cats. I wished Felix all the best. Especially during his continued residence in Illinois. After all, that was a ready solution to our problem. Leave him *behind*.

I presented this idea to Barbara. Felix was her cat. She had raised him from a little ball of fur when he was named, not for Felix the Cat of animated movie fame, but for Felix the Prissy, the meticulous one in *The Odd Couple*.

Barbara was somewhat receptive. "Maybe the neighbor girls would take him," she said. She tried that tactic. No go. It seems the neighbor girls made the mistake of giving their father a vote.

There seemed only one other place to turn for guidance: Felix's personal physician, old doc Floogle, the local vet. Barbara and I agreed to put the question to him of whether or not we would take Felix along.

A rabies shot was the occasion. We drove to the doc's. Barbara set her jaw as she gathered up Felix to go into the office. "Whatever he says goes," she said slowly, through clenched teeth.

We sat down by the examination table. By then I was resigned to it. Too bad. Felix just wasn't the sort to travel. Too old. Too set in his ways. I looked over at Barbara. She had steeled herself. Her eyes stared down. Her lips were tight. "Good," I thought, "she's ready for the bad news."

Which left me quite surprised for the actions which came with the answer. The quivering lower lip, the blinking away of tears, the furtive little pats on Felix's furry head. But not by Barbara.

By the veterinarian!

"You can't leave that cat with someone else!"

Doc Floogle exploded. "He's lived too long with you. Why that would be terrible." He paused. "Get him a little harness and a leash. He'll travel well in a motor home."

Good old Doc Floogle. He can say that, sitting back in his Illinois cornfield counting hogs while we're imprisoned with this beast—in our cage on wheels heading west.

Yet it did calm my fears somewhat. I put a smile on my face and went to the pet store to buy Felix a little harness.

Then the following day I went *back* to the pet store and up to the large blonde woman who sold me the thing. "It's too small."

"Too small for a cat?"

"Yes," I replied. "He's about this big." I indicated his thick neck span with the open hands I had used to measure him. This time.

"Oh, he's a big cat," she agreed. "Here, this one for a dog may do better."

I checked it against my measurements. "Should do. It's his first harness," I mumbled, sounding I suppose like a mother buying her son his first athletic supporter.

"Oh?" the young woman answered, sort of amazed. "Kitty's never worn one before?"

"No, Kitty's..." Now she had me doing it, "the cat has never even seen one before."

She looked at me with reproach. Her eyes even resembled those of a cat expressing severe disdain. "*You're* going to put it on him?"

I nodded.

"Kitty isn't going to like ooou."

The logical next step for this enterprise was: A Test Drive.

That evening, as soon as *Barbara* had wrestled through the arduous labors of putting Felix's harness on him, I broached the subject. "Let's take Felix for a spin in the motor home."

"Good idea." So with the cat hoisted into the vehicle we made a run to the supermarket. The trip there was fine. He stood up in Barbara's lap most of the way watching the landscape go by. He did not look thrilled. On the other hand, he didn't look petrified with fright.

By the time we were finished with our errands it was dark. For our return Felix stationed himself by the rear window of the motor home. As I looked in the rear view mirror I noted that headlights would approach us, then back off a little, then stay for a while. Or pass hurriedly by. A further look in the mirror revealed that Felix had stationed himself by the plastic wide-angle lens stuck on the rear window. Approaching motorists were seeing a strangely distorted cat, somewhat dis-embodied by the edge of the lens. No wonder they took a second look.

◆   ◆   ◆

The day finally came when it was time to leave. To move it out. A bit beyond time actually. We had taken a little too long in preparation. A blizzard had arrived. In a way that was good, though. When moving to what we hoped would be a sunny, warm clime I always like to leave a northern state in a snowstorm. Confirms one's good judgment.

The last item of gear was stowed. We were ready to start our engine and slither onto the snow-covered roadway. Then we began to look for Felix.

No Felix.

High and low. We couldn't find him.

Now how can a cat, a large gray cat, disappear in an *empty* apartment? "Where is the cat?" I asked with what tried to be the voice of calmness and tolerance. "I mean the snow's two feet deep, we're four hours late starting—and no Felix!"

Somehow Barbara had the notion that there was some chance I might not retain my usually placid ways—and lose my temper.

"Good Lord, woman! Where is *your* cat?"

In fairness, it should be pointed out that Felix hates moving as much or more than I do. He had moved a number of times. The sight of cardboard boxes piled in the living room is enough to send him into wide-eyed looks of fear, then fur-tive glances about and, finally, quick darting moves into a place of hiding.

"Here he is!" Barbara shouted from the bathroom. I ran, fearing he might have dreaded moving so much he'd hanged himself from the shower rod. At times I'd considered it myself.

Felix, seemingly shrunken in size, was cowering behind the stool. He had managed to fit into the shape of the fixture and, with his gray fur, blend into the shadows.

"Come on, Felix," I tried, coaxing. At first he wouldn't even look up at us. Then a quick, "Why do you do this to me?" came to his eyes. Soft strokes on him brought his head up. With some pushing and pulling we got him out and we all marched then, with our heads up, to the waiting coach.

I started the engine.

The road opened before us and the vehicle picked up speed. Looks of relief crossed Barbara's face and mine. We both reached out and patted Felix's head for reassurance.

Ours—not his.

2

The Cairo Blues

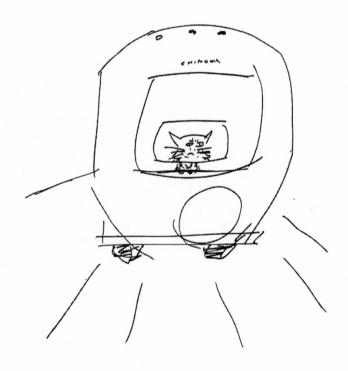

I don't know if there is actually a song, "The Cairo Blues" but there should be.

"Turn on the radio," I said peering vainly through the snow storm in search of the road. "Let's find out when we might run out of this mess." We were headed south, due south. Normally one expects that as one goes in a southerly direction the cold, nasty business will lessen.

Barbara tuned the radio: "The heaviest belt of the storm is in a line just north of Cairo, Illinois. A foot and half are already on the ground there. Another foot is expected."

I shut it off. I didn't need any map to tell me where we were. The eighteen inches of snow we were plowing through—since the snowplows hadn't yet—were enough.

Just north of Cairo.

Cairo is one of those places blessed by the hands of God and man to become an Important City. The mighty Ohio River meets, and miles downstream finally joins, the great Mississippi. The most important river confluence in the United States of America. Geographically, and politically, Cairo is where North meets South; and the Eastern half meets the Western half. Man also took a hand by building the Illinois Central Railroad through on one axis, joining on another axis, the New York Central Railroad.

And what has Cairo done with all this beneficence? Steadfastly dug in its heels and resisted almost every measure for progress. When I first visited Cairo in 1951 it was a sleepy, quaint, dying river town. Today it shows every sign of having gone steadily down hill from there.

On one visit in the '60s I saw a group of well-kept white youths swimming amidst all sorts of filth in the river. I asked them why they swam there when there was a perfectly good swimming pool uptown. In a direct and succinct manner they explained that they'd rather swim in the brown stuff in the river than with the brown people in the pool.

Now, don't misunderstand. Cairo has charm for me. I suppose Charles Dickens saw it at its worst when he viewed it and proclaimed: "That dismal place. That swamp. That Cairo."

I used to view it as a haven, a place of rest on various treks north and south, up and down the Mississippi Valley. I'd stop in the old "Mark Twain" cafe/bar/diner/night club and refresh myself with a cup of coffee or, on a hot July day, a quiet Michelob draft and an American cheese sandwich on rye.

Traveling by any place where one has been before is bound to stir memories. Usually some pleasant nostalgia. Not always though. One daylight nightmare I can never seem to evade is remembrance of an afternoon I spent in Cairo. I sat at the confluence. The point of land where the Ohio River meets the Mississippi. I sat there trying to put my life back together. This visit marked my separation from my second wife. I had just left her, left my home, possibly was on the way to losing my job. I ached with the pain, my head pounding with the grief at the death of all those hopes. Where had it gone awry? What had I done wrong?

Though they didn't seem to so at the time, somehow the flowing waters must have helped. I survived.

That grim day marked one milestone down the trails that now brought Barbara and me to be driving through snow to Cairo.

Barbara had also been through two marriages. For us you might say that moonlight and roses didn't exactly hold the allure they did at age seventeen. Or even twenty-five. The old Hollywood movies didn't ring any bells. "That old black magic" was more like sleight of hand.

On the other hand, slight or not, when the romantic fog blows away, one can generally see what's really there.

Barbara and I had met on a clear day a couple of years before. She was working as a graduate assistant in the archives of Southern Illinois University in Carbondale while finishing her master's degree. I had just arrived in the archives as a recently retired faculty member who had volunteered to help process a collection they had. Louisa, who ran the section where I reported, seemed to pounce on us with a certain purpose—nay, "glee" I should say—as she made the introductions. I think she hoped something good would come of it.

Since the two of us were now rolling westward in a mini motor home it probably doesn't have to be pointed out that something good had come of it.

Sometime about a year before, I had started rumbling on to Barbara about how I was ready to leave and go somewhere else to live. Then at some point, Barbara had pointed out that if I went somewhere else to live without her she'd go somewhere else to live without me. That brought things into focus somewhat. Finally I said, "Let's go and live somewhere else together."

"Ah," Barbara responded, "and you just remembered I have more Duke Ellington records than you do. So which somewhere else do you have in mind for us to go?"

"I've thought some about Portland," I responded.

"Oregon or Maine?" she inquired, beginning to worry a little perhaps about my carefulness in considering a move.

"Either one. They each have a certain charm."

"Does it snow in either one?" she asked.

"Hmm, I'd forgotten about that," I replied. I pondered the situation. "Does it snow in San Diego?" I asked, knowing she'd lived there for awhile.

"Not that I ever heard."

"Let's look at San Diego first," I replied. "Then we can decide."

For Barbara the change had come at a logical point in her life. By then she had finished the work on her degree and had a job in her field—human services. However it was not the job of a lifetime. Her daughter Jenny, son David, and even her son Bob—the one with the big Harley motorcycle—were about as settled as one ever is, into lives of their own. Finally the youngest, Stephen, was ready to leave home. In the autumn of our departure it came time for him to take that step—or be pushed—into the slippery World. Stephen was about to move on to what we call Life. However, with more of mine behind me than ahead, I find occasionally I'd still like to climb back under the covers and have my mom bring me milk toast and tell me everything will be all right.

Because sometimes it won't. "It's a jungle out there, Tarzan."

As for me, I too was at a turning point. After the Second World War helped develop so many uses for 16 mm film, many universities had set up units to make their own educational and documentary films. I was one of the fortunate people blessed with a career there. I worked at several universities over the years and got to make all sorts of films on all sorts of fascinating subjects. But finally a budget squeeze at my recent employer, Southern Illinois University and the eclipse of film by video made my job obsolete. I switched to teaching film courses full-time but early retirement beckoned. I took the money—and now—ran.

The interstate turned off west—to miss Cairo. Fate's final thumb of the nose.

"Where's Felix?" I asked.

"He's asleep on the cushion in back," Barbara replied. "Hey we're almost out of Illinois!"

We climbed slowly onto the Interstate 57 bridge, testing for slipperiness. Nothing—just wetness. We picked up speed—soaring over the Mississippi River like fleeing birds. Or cats, as the case might be.

"Goodbye, Old Man," I said, not without some tightness in my throat.

3

The Bide-a-Wee Motel

Trailer and motor home travelers pride themselves on their self-sufficiency—the ability to stop and have electricity, water, heat, all the amenities of home, provided by the equipment in the motor home itself. However, there comes a time when you travel in such conveyances that you swallow hard, sigh and looking as far down the road as you can, reluctantly murmur, "Let's find a motel."

Peering out through the poor visibility of blowing snow and hastening nightfall I uttered the magic words of resignation to Barbara. We were in northern Arkansas. It was toward the end of the first day of our journey.

Barbara and I. And Felix. All in my motor home, skidding a little on Interstate 55 as the slush and water from the day's precipitation began to freeze. Then snow started to stick. We turned our gaze ahead for a welcoming neon. Under those circumstances my motor home becomes simply a motor vehicle. I am glad to park it—and leave it for the night.

"Glub," I said.

"What is it?" asked Barbara, worried.

"Nothing," I replied, slowing to look at the road's surface—fast disappearing into whiteness. "See any good place to stop?"

"Barely," she answered. "Under the circumstances though, how does the Bide-a-Wee Motel sound?"

"Great!" I agreed.

Felix didn't join our discussion. He just scrunched down between the two bucket seats, probably wishing this moving thing would stop. Soon.

Which it did as I pulled up to the motel office. Finding the path to the office icy, I was glad we'd pulled in. "Bide-a-Wee" or whatever it was called.

The motel was your average, aged, by-the-side-of-the-interstate type. Since the interstate—and the motel—were built, the interstate had been re-done. The motel had not. Except for conversion to color television sets. When color first became widespread—around 1964.

The clerk assigned us a unit down the line. I was glad we'd be a ways away from the office. I've smuggled a few things into motels in my time—no enumeration seems called for at this stage in my life—but never had I smuggled in a cat.

"Do you think we should ask them about taking Felix into the room?" Barbara had inquired earlier.

"Never," I said. "They might say 'no.'" I knew that many motels have a distinct aversion to renting rooms to cats. Cats claw things. They may not use their litter boxes. And worst of all, male cats spray to mark their territory. A squirt here, a squirt there. One time, after a visit by one stray male cat to my apartment, I noticed that the paint dropped off the corners of my furniture. I could understand the motel owners' rules. But I knew Felix wouldn't do any such things. "Besides," I went on, "we couldn't leave him out here in the vehicle tonight. It's not a fit night out for man nor beast."

"Right." Barbara said. "You hold him while I take his things into the room first."

"Where is he?" I asked. From my place at the front I took the flashlight and pointed it into the recesses of the back. Felix was sitting by the back door, waiting to be let out.

"Felix! Felix!" I called. He came. A somewhat unfair diversion to keep him from leaping out the rear door while Barbara went around there to remove and carry into the room his food, food dish, water dish, litter pan, and sleeping blanket.

"It's all in," she shouted from the door. "Bring Felix."

Every time I picked the cat up to carry him out of the motor home to some other overnight abode I had visions of him vaulting from my arms to disappear, say, into the wilds of Arkansas. Or wherever we were, at any given time. An escape not unknown in the feline world. Cats have tremendous strength and leverage. If they don't want to be held in your arms they have ways of not being held in your arms.

Fortunately, Felix just looked around and was soon inside on all fours again. He explored briefly and retreated under the bed.

As I carried in the next load of gear, though, Barbara shouted "Careful!"

"What?"

"You didn't check the door before opening it. Felix might have been waiting to dash out."

"Right," I responded. "I am not used to traveling with a cat."

We soon had everything in and were settled. I turned on the ancient television set. It would be nice to sit back and just watch a little on the tube—instead of staring at streaks of snow blowing straight at us.

Wrong. The screen, when it finally warmed up, had two distinct images. Plus one indistinct one. All in bluish green. Then, occasionally, those images would be interrupted as the whole thing rolled, over and over.

After appropriate macho, male-oriented knob-fiddling I announced that I would go get another room with a decent television. Assuming the Bide-a-Wee had one, of course.

"Okay." Barbara agreed. "Then we'll schlep the stuff to the new room."

I explained the situation to the desk clerk. He replied that we were welcome to try another room but, "Meantime, let me try and see if I can get your set working."

"It won't be necessary," I mumbled. "I mean I'm sure it won't work. Definitely." I could see us getting thrown out on the road—lock, stock and kitty litter.

"Oh, it's no trouble," he smiled. "I'll just give it a shot. Might save you trouble."

I protested. But to no avail.

At the room door I called in, "Barbara, the room clerk is here. He wants to check the TV."

No answer. I could hear some sounds of movement however.

The clerk appeared restless.

"Barbara?"

No reply.

"She must be in the bathroom," I offered.

We waited a few more moments then Barbara came to the door. "I was just putting away some things in the bathroom." Indeed. Felix and equipment were stashed. I just hoped he wouldn't scratch to get out. I was pretty sure he wouldn't meow. Felix doesn't do that much. Hardly ever. Very seldom. Rarely.

He wouldn't dare do that.

Would he?

"You're right; it doesn't work," the clerk said after he knob fiddled a while. "Funny. We haven't had complaints from other customers passing through."

I stifled a desire to point out that Davy Crockett probably hadn't been that interested in television, took the new room key, thanked the man and saw him to the door.

"I didn't expect you to bring *him*," Barbara said as soon as the coast was clear.

"He insisted on trying it," I replied. "And we waited so long I thought you really were stuck in the bathroom."

"No," she said. "It was just that I had to crawl all the way under the bed to get Felix. And he didn't want to budge."

We moved to another room where the television displayed images which were almost recognizable.

Cats seem to seek havens of security whenever they are in a world of change, one not of their making. I recalled Ray and Samantha. Samantha was the felis catus; Ray the homo sapiens. Samantha was a gorgeous, still not quite mature, female Siamese. On *their* first motel stop on the open road, Sammy completely disappeared. Ray, after a frantic search, found her—up inside the bed springs.

Ray had told me since that Samantha learned to love traveling.

The next morning I wished Felix the same as I plopped him into the vehicle. When we pulled onto the highway the sun was trying to push some light through high overcast clouds. No more snow had come. In fact what was there was melting. And there was the hint of warmth in the air.

We were at the point where we made a right turn—from going south to going west. Westward Ho!

We were definitely on our way.

4

A Song is Born?

Who would dare to try and top the lyrics to that popular melody about getting one's exhilaration, or as they put it, "kicks," on a certain highway numbered sixty-six? I mean you can try, but "Let's get sporty on Interstate Forty" simply will not do. Not in the same league. So Barbara and I gave up before we started.

In fact we were turning away from the musically acclaimed high spots of route 66. We weren't even going to Amarillo, Albuquerque and Winslow. Instead we were going to cut south at Little Rock and aim for Pecos, El Paso and Tucson. Much as we would liked to have stopped in central New Mexico and perhaps nipped up to Santa Fe, the southernmost route seemed less likely to bring chances of more snow and ice. So it was Interstate 40, Interstate 30 and Interstate 20 for us. Hmm. How about, "It's a land of plenty when you roll on Twenty?"

Okay. Never mind.

In the meantime we had not left snow entirely behind but the surface of highway 40 was nearly dry, well into Arkansas. We passed a sign to Village Creek State Park and recalled a pleasant mid-winter campsite in the woods there.

"You remember the signs in the next town?" Barbara asked.

"How could I forget?" I replied. A laundromat stop there had revealed that the local merchants had put warning signs in their windows. However instead of, "Trespassers Found on These Premises Will be Prosecuted" they all read, "Trespassers Found on These Premises Will be Shot."

Barbara commented: "Judge Roy Bean must have paused there on his way to Texas."

We kept on rolling. Through the morning and into the afternoon. The sun and, by now, the balmy gulf winds warmed the land and the air.

So far Felix seemed to be accepting the trip.

But we thought we detected some lack of approval in his manner. Originally we had speculated that Felix would ride out the journey on the cushioned seats in the back. There he could gaze out the window, or recline on his little orange blanket, placed there for just such slumbers. If not, perhaps he would do as he had done on a trial run or two: select the lap of whoever was the passenger to poke a few "I'm making my bed" claw holes into and then settle down, curl up and snooze.

No. What Felix did that day—and forever after on the trip—was to hunker down on the transmission hump between the two bucket seats in the cab. When feeling really pressed he'd go further and stick his head under the passenger seat. We discussed this whole thing (with each other, not with Felix) but never did arrive at a satisfactory answer. Maybe it was the warmth from the machinery in the hump. Or the vibration. I theorized that it was the fact that it was the lowest spot he could find in the moving vehicle. He wanted to be as close to terra firma as possible. Barbara pooh-poohed my theory. And of course Felix wasn't talking—just glancing up now and then from his cramped, noisy quarters with a quick dirty look. Reflecting back on all this now, though—on how he stayed at our sides during the first month after we'd settled into our *final* locale—perhaps he just wanted to be near us.

"Maybe we should find a spot for lunch and give Felix a walk," I suggested.

"Good idea," Barbara agreed.

We found a well-mannered country road away from the interstate. Its shoulders were lines of red clay soil. Thickets clad in autumn colors banked away from there to woods beyond.

It was a shirtsleeve day. We gloried in it.

"Do you want to take him?" Barbara generously offered.

"No," I demurred. "Why don't you? I need to check the oil."

There's no question about it. Since the very first motor-powered vehicle went creeping down the road, men have been checking the oil. Even before that, come to think of it. Of course. They had to "Go check the horses." For, I'd say decades even, this male dodge for avoiding one task or another has worked like a charm. Women were brought to understand that, in general, the mechanical world was not for them. Except of course for washing machines, vacuum cleaners, sewing machines, refrigerators, stoves, and other trivial mechanisms.

Lately, though, I've noticed that women have begun checking oil. "I'll go check the oil, dear. You do the dishes."

It's almost out of control.

"Why don't I check it instead," Barbara offered. "You take Felix."

"Uh," I stammered, "it's just that I'd—I need to check the—the brake fluid too."

"Oh," she slowly responded. "Oh."

I had her there. But I could tell it was just a matter of time until…

Felix was placed in his harness and on his leash. He walked without hesitation. In fact he marched right toward a thicket—where *we* couldn't go. He proved what we feared. He wanted to Go Away. He couldn't be steered; he couldn't be diverted. He just marched. Away. Barbara would pick him up and point him another direction. One, two—away he'd go. He really didn't care which direction he went as long as it was the opposite of the motor home.

I took over walking him for a while—the oil and brake fluids all being fine, thank you. With no more luck. Point him, let loose of his body and away he'd march, pulling full-strength against his harness and leash. "Away, away," he seemed to say.

Fortunately we didn't take his trying to leave us personally. Just snatched his little body out of the bushes, ripped off his harness, thrust his furry hide through the door and dumped him on the floor of the motor home.

Actually we held him and tried to soothe his passion for escape. He obviously *did* want to leave. So we wanted to calm him as much as possible into some kind of traveling truce.

But we never drove with the windows open. We figured Felix would, as sure as God made little white rutabagas, jump out.

As we neared the day's destination, Felix started something he was to do on nearly every day of our journey. Seeming to sense that the open road was about to cease, he stood up, rear paws on the passenger's lap, forepaws on the dash or window sill and peered out. It was like he was checking out our choice of resting spots. I don't think he was trying to wrest away control of the wheel. However...

5

There Are No Boxcars in Heaven

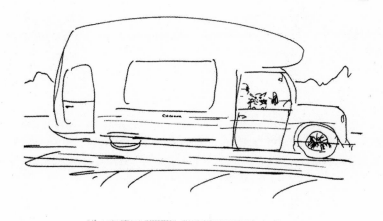

The next day as we rolled on westward we found ourselves in the quaintly named town of Texarkana, tagged for the two states parts of it occupy. Barbara wondered aloud if there were many other places with split names.

"Well, there is Calexico and Mexicali on the California Mexico border," I said. "There's even a song about the latter." I cleared my throat. "So how about a few bars of 'Mexicali Rose'?"

Barbara didn't even give me more than a terse, "No." She went on, "I suppose it's merciful that we're spared such things as Wyontana and Coloansas," she replied.

"Yeah, but someone could probably work up a ditty like 'Texarkana Hanna'," I added.

This got no response whatsoever. However as we proceeded out of town Barbara added, "Anyway, I thought by the time we got to Texas we'd be seeing more RVs heading south for the winter."

"Me too."

"Maybe lots of folks wait until after the Christmas holidays," she said. A supposition we later confirmed.

Despite this shortage of traffic, we all know that many times on the highways one can be inundated with recreational vehicles. Often very large ones.

Our motor home was modest. It was a little Chinook, nineteen feet long and was aptly dubbed a micro-mini in the motor home world. However it had small versions of the necessities: a tiny gas refrigerator, stove, a sink and marine type toilet. It also had gasoline left at the end of the day; the small Toyota engine was not the gas eater the big rigs have. It is somewhat uplifting to pull up alongside a large motor home at a stop light and have the driver ask me, "What mileage you get with that?" When I tell him, "Around nineteen," the look of pain on his face is sometimes too much to bear.

One other aspect of RV travel we found was the freedom for eating. With a fridge on board we could stop where and when we pleased for lunch. No hunting for highway exits jammed with the fast-food eateries blanketing America. Rest stops or even quiet country lanes made lunch a time for picnic-style treats.

After our midday meal that day in a small city park, we discovered a new aspect of life with Felix. Barbara decided to put him in his harness for a last walk before imprisonment. As they walked, a park caretaker started a power mower. Felix hates the sounds of garbage trucks—and lawnmowers. Come to think of it, I don't much care for the sound of lawnmowers either; I avoid them at every opportunity. Felix took exception by crouching to the ground—and ducking out of his harness. Only much faster than the telling takes. Off to the bushes he went.

Now that we knew he could do that, the rest of our trip was to be a little more cautious. Our main hope—a slim one to be sure—was that Felix might not remember his little trick.

Some food managed to lure him from the bushes and we were soon rolling again. We began the long trail across the many miles of the great state of Sam Houston, Jim Bowie, and Tex Ritter. Some unkind soul had carefully informed us that El Paso is closer to San Diego than it is to Texarkana.

"What's on the radio?" Barbara asked, somewhat innocently.

"You know what's on the radio," I replied. "You've been in Texas before."

"Maybe I can find something else," she offered.

"Go ahead," I challenged. Just try."

She did. Try. For some time. Up the FM dial. Down the AM dial.

Only one type of music came to our ears, except when relieved by some cacophonic commercials. Now I know a lot of people—a whole lot of people—not just my fellow Americans but rural Swedes and down-home Czechs and jeanclad Frenchmen—like country western music. Or bluegrass, or "Opry," or Cowboy—whatever you call it. In fact when I was a lad we Iowa youths used to call it "hillbilly." And that could have been the pot calling the kettle a dark name. But we did anyway. So I grew up listening to it. On occasion.

But then I became allergic.

My aversion may have grown from an experience years ago. An overdose.

A 1946 Army leave at Christmas time found me on a free ride from Denver to the aforementioned corn state of Iowa. During the long trip across Nebraska (some wag has pointed out that *any* trip across Nebraska is a "long trip"), I found myself closed up in this fellow's coupe automobile. I do recall that back then we did use the pronunciation, "coo pay." Sounds more elegant than something as confining as "coup." However cooped up we were, listening to the only thing he wanted from his magic Motorola car receiver: the twang of country western music. I heard old favorites like, "Daddy Took My Dog, Away." I didn't get that right. It's: "Dahhdy Tuk Ma Dawawgh Awhay." Or that classic, "I Get Tears in My Ears From Lying on My Back Crying Over You." Or something like that. Even one called, "There Are No Boxcars in Heaven." A reference I suppose to some hope that hobos and the like would be better treated in that big railroad yard up above.

On that Nebraska trip my driver's radio sucked in everything from "Ogallala Olga and Her Rocky Mountain Roundup Girls" to "Sioux City Slim and his Cowpie Wranglers." By the time I got to Ames I could hardly face another diet of saddle sore symphonies.

In that era, finding country western music on the dial was somewhat spotty. Not as spotty as I would have liked but…Nowadays it seems universal, even occupying a fair number of frequencies on the radios of drivers clacking down unwestern landscapes like, say, Connecticut's Merritt Parkway.

But Barbara and I were in the heart of cowboy country. And I was prepared. "Get out the cassettes," I announced.

Along with so many fellow travelers wishing to resume control over our audio inputs, I had shopped for a suitable books-on-tape cassette to carry us from the outskirts of Ft. Worth to somewhere west of El Paso. A book that would not be too serious, one of charm and a degree of humor. I selected readings from the pen of James Herriot of *All Creatures Great and Small* fame. I reasoned that it should be enjoyable to hear tales of a veterinarian in rural Yorkshire while traversing rural Texas.

I made a couple of errors. I failed to reckon on the noise level inside the Chinook. The creaking, the rattles, the wind whistling around the windows made any sound—even outpourings about "San Antone"—difficult to hear with any clarity. On top of that, though, I had picked out a tape recorded by the author himself, the pseudonymous Dr. Herriot, and his thick, was it a Glasgow? accent. His reading is quite charming in the quiet of your living room. Just right for the warm tales he tells. But in the clatter of the Chinook? No. We listened for a whole side of one cassette, pretending to understand. I even chuckled in a few places thinking I'd heard something funny. Finally, when it clicked off, Barbara turned to me, "What was he talking about?"

"Didn't you understand?" I said.

"No," she said simply.

"Well, there was this story about…" I offered lamely.

"About what?" she pressed.

"Well I heard some words that sounded like 'sheep.'" I answered valiantly. I mean I was responsible for picking out and buying the cassette.

"And what else?" she continued.

"Then there was a story about a big dog," I replied. "I think it was a dog."

Silence filled the cab. Even Felix looked up from his transmission nest, curious.

"Is that the only tape you have?" Barbara asked.

"Yes," I replied. "I thought…"

"But we still have to get through New Mexico and Arizona."

"There's one station in Arizona that used to play Big Band music," I announced.

"That was probably in 1948," Barbara retorted.

More silence. Felix pushed his head under the seat.

Finally Barbara said, "Why don't I try the radio again?"

Click.

"Ah knew from the stahrt we'd come to the pahrt where yoooud break ma hahrt. In tew."

That song had ended and several other too before we rolled into Denton, Texas, to stay with old friends. Besides accommodations, Kris and Don promised we'd go to a special Tex-Mex restaurant for a true Southwest food experience. They did. It was.

6

Is Your Cat a Republican?

I don't know if you are aware of the fact that there are Republican cats and Democratic cats.

How, you may ask, a note of disbelief in your voice, can I tell the difference? Or, more to the point, *why* should I?

The why is obvious, Would you want your cat to miss out on his or her Lincoln Day Dinner just because *you* didn't know the cat's political preference? Not to mention dropping disparaging remarks about Millard Fillmore in front of a cat whose deeply felt beliefs were not apparent to you.

You'd better find out—and fast—which way your cat would vote. If cats had the vote. And the way things are going, that may be just around the corner.

Of course all sorts of cutesy comments about cats' political alliances can be brought up. Like: Republican cats are the ones with fur coats. Or: Democratic cats howl a lot. If you serve liver, the cat that goes for it is a Democrat; Republican cats hold out for pâté.

Basically it comes down to considering: Are cats political creatures? There's no room for doubt in that. Anyone at all who has even heard a committee meeting of cats—held in the backyard on a summer night—knows exactly what sort of group they bring to mind.

A friend of mine, a liberal I should note, lived with a cat named Boris. At that time the voting age in Iowa, where they both lived, was eighteen. When Boris reached that age my friend considered taking him down to register to vote. "But," Dick commented, "I realized Boris would vote Republican—and then I just would have to have him put to sleep."

Felix, our travelling companion on the westward sojourn is a fairly conservative cat. If Felix were a person he'd wear gray suits. As a matter of fact, as a cat he wears a gray suit. Except for some streaks of white—including white paws. He looks like a repressed conservative. One who's about to throw over the calm exterior, put on white spats and gloves—then start dancing, while belting out, "Mammy."

Other than that, Felix is sedate. Physically he's about ten inches high, twenty inches long and weighs in at around twelve pounds. He has some Persian Blue in him, judging by appearances. He is a neutered male—which probably explains why he's sedate.

He's more than that though; he's a polite cat. Probably the politest cat I've ever known. Now some cats are haughty; they just ignore you. They go do whatever they want with barely a, "Buzz off, Mac," in your direction. Then there are the loud cats, always clamoring for attention—or telling jokes at the top of their voices. You know that type.

Felix shows none of that behavior. When he wants to eat he doesn't go screaming into the kitchen. He just goes and sits quietly by his food dish. Doesn't utter a peep. Or when he wants to go out, he just sits by the door. No meows. Just an occasional look at a person, if one is nearby, as a quiet request for an exit.

I like to think of it as Conditioned Response. Like old Pavlov and his dog. When Felix wants back in the house, he just takes one paw and rattles the door. When I hear the sound I get up obediently, go to the door and open it. Perfect conditioned response. Sometimes if I do it fast enough Felix will even give me a "Good Boy" look as he marches in. Talk about training.

Now if Felix wants something in the early morning hours before waking—before our waking—his tactics differ. First of all he ignores Barbara. He knows no amount of conditioning will work. Some humans just can't be trained. Hopeless. He knows he'll have to work on me. First of all he sits by the head of the bed and stares at me. That works more often then you'd think. Somehow being stared at, even in deep slumber, then opening one groggy eye—to see two yellow ones fixed on you—does something to the brain. Stirs it.

If that fails, Felix takes one paw and claws lightly around my pillow. Coming out of a sound sleep to find your pillow with claws in it tends to rouse one even faster than the staring treatment.

Sometimes, both approaches having been tried, Felix resorts to his last trick. Especially if he wants outdoors badly enough. Mind you, I sleep face down. Felix, taking all this into account, simply leaps though the air and lands with all four feet right in the middle of my back. *Whopp.* Somehow that never fails to wake me up. Sure fire. *Whopp.*

Times like that though I'm sure he's a Democrat.

All this is how Felix behaves under a normal roof with four walls. A house. We didn't know how he'd do on the road yet. This was our first night, on this trip in the motor home.

And our first in it with Felix.

We were settled in at the Bide-a-Wee Trailer Village and RV Park somewhere near Abilene, Texas. On the old Chisholm Trail. And it was cold on the old Chisholm trail. The wind came whirling down from somewhere in the Colorado Rockies—it felt like—and surrounded our little capsule. We settled in for the night. We didn't like to think that Felix was traveling cabin class but we did assign him to the cab. First of all by our rules Felix does not sleep in human beds. No way. He sleeps by himself, on his little blanket, in other rooms. So we put his food dish and his water dish up in the front and draped his little blanket atop the passenger seat. Barbara somewhat indecorously shoved Felix though the curtain to the cab and we all said goodnight.

Sometime in the small morning hours the wind chilled even more. Now, I thought, it's coming all the way from Montana.

Apparently the gas line to our little furnace felt the chill even more. It froze.

We burrowed deeper into the blankets, trying to keep warm and in place. Doing anything to avoid getting up and confronting the problem directly.

"My feet are cold," Barbara said softly.

"Mine too," I mumbled. "Can we reach any more blankets?" I asked hopefully, but knowing what the grim answer likely was.

"No," Barbara murmured. "Try and get back to sleep."

We tunneled even deeper.

Now, in our small motor home, the bed is made up across the seats by a table top, bridging the aisle and supporting the bed's middle cushions. Underneath us then is a tunnel.

Pushing under the dividing curtain from the cab—and into the tunnel—came Felix. He was I suppose, cold himself. And lonely. And very likely unhappy—having been yanked out of his happy home and transported to the middle of Texas—on a trip where he didn't even have a vote. Democrat or not.

Whopp! Felix was on the bed. At this juncture Barbara and I were cold enough and sleepy enough that we didn't want to enter into a discussion with Felix as to whether or not he might sleep on our bed.

First he choose to settle down between us. Now he could sleep on the bed; I'd concede that. But I didn't relish the idea of reaching over, in the dark, to embrace—a cat.

He got rousted from that spot. Fast.

Then, lo and behold, he wandered down to the foot of the bed and placed his warm little body next to our freezing feet. We had discovered a furry foot warmer. All three of us nodded off to dreamland. For all the remaining days and weeks of our winter trek Felix had earned a place in our hearts. And minds. And lower extremities.

7

Museum Collecting

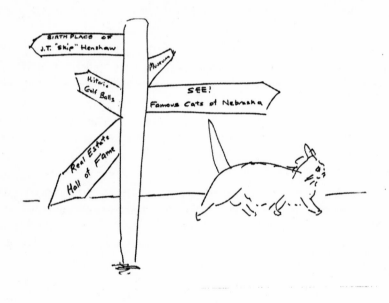

We left Abilene on a clear sun-filled day. It was a day to raise one's spirits. It reminded me that this was not just a trek to get from Point A to Point S; it was also a vacation. A junket to enjoy. A trip.

I've always loved to travel. Perhaps because I got an early start. In 1926 when I was only four months old my parents loaded me in our new Buick and I bounced my way westward on the Lincoln Highway—from Iowa to the mountains of Estes Park, Colorado. It was my father's idea. Actually it turned out he didn't drive with my mother, brother and me on that rough, dusty roadway. He took the train. I mean there *are* limits. Though he liked travel, my father's tolerance for discomfort was not very high. I later followed in his footsteps but on that early trip, I didn't have much choice.

Not that my father was always above taking the wheel. I recall a trip in our new 1938 Buick. We were sliding over icy roads on our way back from a Christmas visit to Niagara Falls. I had been given a toy xylophone—which I dutifully hammered away at in the back seat. My father, though he would engineer family trips, chose to distance himself from domestic trials. He turned to my mother and said, "Would you tell him to stop that?" I got the message. In fact that ended my musical career. To this day I've never touched another xylophone.

I've touched many a roadmap though. Worn them out. However I'm not the sort of traveler who makes much of driving just "to get there." For example, I once made a trip to Montana with friends. The first day when I announced it was time to stop for lunch one passenger, Grace, thought I was joking: "Stop for lunch? I never heard of such a thing." It seems her husband would simply start out in the morning and *go*.

After that trip—and the kind of off-the-track, side lunch trips I made—Grace was ruined forever. In fact on that trip Grace got to the point of picking lunch spots herself. Even to take one of our side trip meanderings to the Stratobowl in South Dakota. It was there in the 1930s that the National Geographic Society and the U.S. Army launched some of the first men in space. They went up to 60,613 feet, hanging in a tiny gondola below a forty story high balloon. The reason the bowl was used is that it is a natural indentation in the earth, deep enough to shelter the tall balloons from the wind during inflation. A unique place in American history.

My interest then is in traveling to explore. As for "getting down the road" my record—in an inverse sort of way—is one day when the total progress measured seventeen miles.

I especially like to poke into local museums. I see something on the map in small red type that says "Riverboat Museum" (say, a museum on the towboat

George M. Verity in Keokuk, Iowa) and I'm a hopeless case. I'll follow any back street. A battered, faded sign: "City Museum; 8 blks." and I'm off the main drag and in pursuit. A muffled mention of the "Corn Palace" in Mitchell, South Dakota, will set my eyes to eagerly searching for an interstate exit.

Originally I think I got hooked into this in Marietta, Ohio. The Campus Martius Museum there has such a distinct local flavor. The two-hundred-year-old Rufus Putnam home and the displays of articles used by earlier citizens of Marietta speak so eloquently of the rich history of this Ohio community. That is the special quality of smaller, local museums. They convey the spirit of their place in a way that large, more sophisticated ones don't.

I guess you might say I "collect" such places. Not all of them—just some, selected by fancy. It's true that I have a leaning toward river spots. So much of this country was built by people traversing our waterways.

Then too certain treasures in cities come to mind. One gem I recall is Sweden House, actually the "American Swedish Institute," in Minneapolis. It is a handsome museum in what was the mansion of Swan Turnblad, the publisher of *Svenska Amerikanska Posten,* an important organ in Minnesota history. The day Barbara and I were there a group of visitors from Sweden were on tour. With all those Swedes and fair-haired Barbara around I began to notice I was the only person in the whole house with brown eyes.

In Springfield, Illinois, before the National Park Service surrounded Lincoln's house with a complete and charming reconstructed neighborhood, the house simply sat there by itself. Back then, when I first visited it, the backyard outhouse was roped off. "What for?" I asked. "Archeologists are digging for artifacts," I was informed. That made me think of how Mr. Lincoln would have probably laughed about that. I could see him up in Heaven, nudging Senator Douglas and saying, "Look down there in Springfield—where those damn fools are digging now. What next?"

In my "collection" real places truly excite me. Usually, reconstructions don't. I know there's a lot of authenticity to Colonial Williamsburg and thousands—millions?—of people go there each year. But I feel manipulated. The place has the feel of being "Precious." Orchestrated. It was as if that was where Walt Disney first got his big idea. I realize this will surely cinch my being persona non grata in Williamsburg. But I'm in trouble there anyway ever since I questioned, aloud, to the management, why a reconstructed tavern didn't actually serve alcoholic beverages. I mean why did we fight the Revolution anyway?

But to stand on the plain grassy earth at Yorktown where the British, in their fine uniforms, marched away in defeat—that stirs my blood. While there I wondered if the haughty English had ever given a passing thought to the idea that, perhaps unlike Waterloo, the battle of Yorktown had been lost on the playing fields of Eton.

Then in Scottsbluff, Nebraska, there are the cuts in the rock left by the wagons as they rolled westward. They give me a run of goose bumps too. And to stand across from the mouth of the Missouri River, near Alton, Illinois, where Meriwether Lewis and William Clark stood before pushing off on their noble trip of exploration heats the tempo of my pulse.

Our American history is all so new. I once pointed out the old cathedral in St. Louis to a visitor from Prague, Czechoslovakia. He found it of interest but it also amused him to point out that the apartment building he lived in at home was older.

Of course I think the recentness is one of the things that generates excitement in visiting some special spot of history. A few years ago I was in Asheville, North Carolina. There I had a whole afternoon to reverently tour the house where Thomas Wolfe had grown up—and which he chronicled so well in *Look Homeward Angel*. Because his mother—and her retinue of boarders—were there long after Wolfe's death, the house never was owned by anyone but her. The lamps, the furniture—the smells—were still as she left them, as Wolfe recalled them so vividly on paper. Unfortunately, since my visit, a fire in part of the house must have taken away some of that atmosphere forever.

I realize, in this short list of my "collection" that I shouldn't be so scornful of reconstructions. The rebuilding of Ft. Michilimackinae in Mackinaw City, Michigan, thoroughly captivated Barbara and me on a recent visit there. Perhaps it's because the excitement of the "dig" and the energy of the people working on the reconstruction conveyed an aliveness to us. I still carry a very vivid picture in my mind of what it must have been like to have been stationed in that remote, snow-bound outpost. I recall one item—written up in the literature at the fort—which pointed out that the isolated living conditions so deranged one footsoldier that he had an affair with a lieutenant's wife. A dangerous pursuit even in the best of times.

On our westward odyssey, as Barbara steered us down Interstate 20, 1 carefully scrutinized the map of west Texas. Ah! I found something in small red type.

"Would you like to take a look at the Permian Basin Petroleum Museum in Midland?" I asked.

"What if I even tried to say no?" came the reply.

As if I didn't hear, I continued, "Here's how we get there. First we look for Exit 136, then…"

8

All Aboard

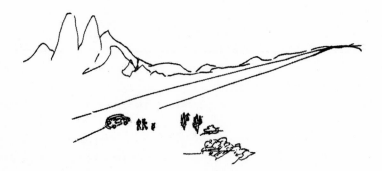

That evening I could see a glow from the lights of El Paso brightening the sky. Of course in the Midwest when you see a city's lights you are close to it; the hazier air does that. In the West those clear nighttime skies announce a town far in advance. The glow hangs there over long distances. It's like seeing the "clouds" on the horizon while driving in the flat lands of Colorado. Then you realize that the "clouds" are actually the white peaks of the Rocky Mountains. Then you think, "I'll be there before long." But you're wrong.

I put this into words: "I always seem to forget how big these western skies are."

"Yes," Barbara replied.

"And how much I miss them," I went on. "Also seeing trains in the big open space. Where you can see the whole long line of a hundred-car freight train slipping across the landscape. Too far away to hear. And looking small in the scale of the country around it."

I reflected on that. "Speaking of trains, did I ever tell you about my experience with the United Nations train in Oregon?" I inquired.

"No," Barbara responded.

The tale came from an encounter in the summer of 1945. 1 was in the West then too, in The Dalles, Oregon, on the Columbia River, east of Portland.

It was an era when, for their evening's entertainment, Americans would actually go down to the depot and watch the train come in. At least they—we—did it in smaller towns where there was little else to do in the leisure hours before bedtime. The event was somewhat like the arrival and departure of an ocean liner. Especially in the West with its vast distances and far apart towns.

I was in The Dalles with my friend Jim. We had been sent there by the U.S. Department of Agriculture. We were dubbed Pear Psylla Scouts. For our scouting patrols we were even assigned an official government USDA truck. We had taken the summer away from college to join battle against this bug. The pear psylla was about the size of a pin head, but it had destroyed the pear orchards of the East. It was feared it could do the same to those in the Northwest.

Our job was to find the insects by using sticky boards—like flypaper—so spray crews could be dispatched to dispatch the creatures. Prior to using traps, the scouts like us had tracked their prey *visually.* If you think that peering up into a pear tree to spot something only slightly larger than a flying flea was absurd—you're right.

In arid areas around The Dalles the pear trees were few and far between. And as far as we could tell, the pear psylla were non existent.

After our daily "patrols," Jim and I would return to town, clean up—it took white gas to dissolve the sticky stuff from our hands—and consume a fresh salmon dinner at the Columbia Cafe. Then we'd repair to our hotel room to dash off quick letters to parents and friends. We timed it all so we could meet the Union Pacific Portland Limited at 8:20. The train was Chicago bound and carried a railway mail car. Those cars, had clerks in them to sort the mail as the train crossed the country. Our letters, dropped in a slot in the car's side, would be delivered in Ames, Iowa, three days later. Faster than now I'd bet.

Jim and I would then join the townsfolk who were on hand to greet the Limited. It did not linger long; if anyone ever got off it was usually just someone returning from Portland.

One night though, a new excitement was added to train watching. The United Nations had just been formed in San Francisco and we all knew that the key delegates and ambassadors had been whisked through The Dalles earlier that day on a train tour across the United States. The national news told of this gift tour of the United States given by this country to the new UN. But the Associated Press barely mentioned that a second UN train, bearing the administrative assistants, secretaries—all the people who probably made things run—was close behind. Maybe just in case some big shot had to stop and dictate an urgent memo.

Anyway, the second train temporarily halted its overland journey in The Dalles. It's huge steam locomotive had a cracked wheel. They had to change it. I'd never seen the likes. Neither had most the population of The Dalles, which began to arrive in droves. We all watched the crew jack up the engine and replace the wheel. Like changing an auto tire. Only this vehicle weighed 200 tons. So the whole procedure took a while. Naturally all the UN people left the train. There were Chinese and French and Russians and Indians and Australians all over the platform. Actually all over the town. There were the costumes and colors and languages of the world there. The UN had invaded The Dalles.

Finally, the wheel replaced, it was time to leave. The whistle tooted its demanding command. The call, "All aboard," echoed down the platform. Even before then, the train crew had obviously been strained to the limits to try and keep a semblance of order in this Babel. Now they had to round up their wandering charges. They explained as best they could in English that it was, "Time to go again."

One exasperated conductor approached Jim and me. In slowly formed words he said, "Time-to-get-on-train. We-go." Looking about me, I realized that Jim and I—in our sports coats, shirts and slacks—looked like the UN crowd, not the more informally attired local people.

"All-aboard," the conductor ordered us again. "Return-to-the-train."

The idea hit like a flash. We could get on and probably go all the way to Washington, D.C.. Pretend not to spikk Angliss. Just move around the train a lot. It was probably just one unending party anyway.

The chance of a lifetime. What an experience!

Then a porter came along and also tried to herd us aboard.

I looked at Jim and he looked at me.

We both sort of said in unison, "No. We work here."

Somehow we figured the whole thing would be extremely difficult to explain to the U.S. Department of Agriculture.

But I've always wondered.

What if...

9

Crossing the Pecos

For the next stop on our westward trip we camped at Monahans Sandhills State Park near Monahans, Texas. The following morning before departure I decided to give Felix some exercise. Prior to "lockup." What I didn't know was that Felix had the same notion for me—exercise. Held back only by the harness and leash, away he went, marching up the first mound of sand dunes. Then down, and up the next rise. Nothing swayed him, nothing swerved him. He was on the move. He looked like a member of the French Foreign Legion seeking the Lost Patrol.

I thought I'd just keep following—to see when he'd slacken the pace. Up another dune and down. Felix didn't let up. He kept eyes straight ahead, marching on. He was headed for Mexico. At his present rate it looked like he'd be halfway to the Rio Grande by dinner time. Dinner time for some Pecos County coyote.

At the top of the next high dune I looked back. The Chinook was small in the distance. Felix—and I—had covered considerable territory.

"Enough, Felix," I said, as if that would make any difference. I finally restrained him by pulling the harness tight against his chest. Remembering how easily he had slipped out of the harness earlier, I reached down and picked him up.

Felix did not want to go back. He liked Monahans Sandhills. Or he hated being locked up, one. Anyway we headed back over hill, over dale—Felix kicking most of the way.

"Felix, it's for your own good," I reassured him. He gave me a couple of shoves with his hind feet to make sure I knew he didn't like the message. Bondage was not his style.

Finally back at the starting point, I opened the top half of the Chinook's rear door, a Dutch door, and dumped Felix's quivering little body inside.

"There."

"You and Felix must have had a nice long trek," Barbara commented, laughing.

I didn't find it quite that amusing. Marching up and down soft sand dunes where one's shoes sink in on every step is not my idea of fun. "Yes," I said, tersely. "Next stop you take him. I ought to be using this time to check the oil."

The West of the Pecos Museum in historic Pecos turned out to be a pleasant stop. It was in the old Orient Hotel. The restored barroom was intact even down to a hole near the door where one .45 slug had left its mark in a gunfight. It seems that John Denson and Bill Earhart had threatened to kill Barney Riggs. Barney took the first counter action that came to mind. He drew and fired. Cartridges exploded and John and Bill said goodbye to this world on the floor at the Orient's saloon.

As we rolled into the Apache Mountains west of Pecos it seemed the appropriate time to pin on my tin "Pecos, Texas" star given to me at the museum. We were truly in the Old West. I went in the back, rummaged around, got out my old gray Stetson hat left to me by my Uncle Dan. Dan hadn't lived in Texas; he lived in San Francisco and had bought the hat to wear in a parade, I guess. At least that's what his sister, my Aunt Ruth, had told me a few years ago when she gave me the ten-gallon headpiece. Just after she had presented me with the hat I placed it on my head. "Hey," I said going for a mirror, "don't I look like Tom Mix?"

My aunt, carefully scrutinizing my rotund shape, gray mustache and little white goatee, said quickly, "No. Not really. As a matter of fact you look more like Colonel Sanders."

Now as we hurried down the highway I returned to the passenger seat, decorated with badge and hat, and said, "Here we are—in the wild wooly west. Yahoo!"

Barbara turned her eyes abruptly away from the road for a look. Then back to the road. "Don't do that to me while I'm driving!"

Earlier, when we had crossed the flat, sandy, gravelly area that in a wetter season would be the Pecos River, I reflected that we were almost exactly half way on our trek. Carbondale to the Pacific. Or Bust.

10

Outlaws

Reflecting on the wild west and its collection of outlaws I am struck by the color-ful quality of the nicknames given these mavericks: the Pecos Kid, Billy the Kid, Calamity Jane, Wild Bill Hickok, Curly Bill Brocius.

Curly Bill incidentally originated a clever bit of business known as the Curly Bill Toss. If someone calls on one to surrender one's revolver, one places the fire-arm in the palm of one's hand, butt end toward the person making this demand. Then one holds it out toward the other party. As one does so, one puts one's trig-ger finger inside the trigger guard and quickly, very quickly, flips the gun upright so it has the business end now pointing toward the person who wishes to disarm one. In Bill's case with an old single-action revolver he also had to fan the ham-mer of the gun back with the palm of his other hand. As one did all this, one pulled on the trigger, firing the piece, and possibly eliminating the source of the ill-conceived request.

It is apparently a fact that Bill used this trick once on Marshal Fred White. Bill said his gun went off accidentally. Deputy Marshal Wyatt Earp disputed that and whacked Bill over the head with his own pistol. From his deathbed White agreed with Bill and the latter was set free.

It is not known now if Curly Bill used this maneuver much but apparently he didn't have to, considering the widespread knowledge in Tombstone of Bill's, if I may put it this way, hair-trigger temper.

However, in my childhood era of the 1930s we too had a goodly number of outlaws with lively monikers: Pretty Boy Floyd, Mad Dog Coll, Machine Gun Kelly, Ma Barker. It was sort of the "Wild Midwest." Newspapers never called it that but they didn't mind what stories about these "desperadoes" did for their cir-culations.

The biggest stories of all were about the one man who never had a nickname. John Dillinger. He was Public Enemy Number One on the "G-Men's" list.

On top of that though, Dillinger had a certain show business appeal. His combed-back hair and lopsided, infectious grin certainly resembled someone who became a later-day star, Humphrey Bogart. Dillinger also had something a lot of people had lost in the Depression: a sense of humor. While running from the Indiana State Police he'd call their chief now and then to "check in." Fleeing from one Iowa bank robbery, with hostages hanging all over the getaway car, one elderly woman asked to get off. They were approaching her home. Dillinger stopped to oblige.

Don't get me wrong. Shirley Temple he wasn't. But Dillinger really seemed to dislike shooting people. Robbing banks, yes. Hurting people, no. In fact, looking at it from my perspective now I would feel safer sitting down with Dillinger then wandering into one of today's drug-gang neighborhoods.

In fact he was viewed as somewhat of a folk hero. After all, who did he rob? Banks. And who were the villains? The places that foreclosed mortgages on thousands of farmers and others having a very tough time in the Depression. The Banks.

One day, though, after all the rampaging headlines and gangster capers, Dillinger's game seemed to play out. His roaming and robbing stopped. The news heads announced: "Dillinger Nabbed." They had him. For sure. In the "jug."

Or did they?

"Dillinger Beats Rap. Escapes." Here we go again! That jazzed things up. The story I heard was that he scared the guards with a fake gun he'd carved out of a potato. Must have been bigger potatoes in that jail than we had at my house.

Then he was everywhere. Someone even pointed out to me that a secluded cabin on a Minnesota lake was, "one of Dillinger's hideaways." Even at fifteen cents a gallon, just to buy the gas to go from all the hideaways where he "lay low" to all the banks he "stuck up" must have used up most of his ill-gotten gains.

It had to be just a matter of time before he showed up in my home town. After all, we were in the middle of Iowa. He couldn't miss.

In fact, one tale was that he probably was the one who robbed our State Bank a couple of years before. Of course no self-respecting Iowa town was going to have its bank robbed by just some yahoo who wandered in out of the dust of the Lincoln Highway.

Only *Dillinger* would do if you were to hold up your head with any degree of civic pride.

Then one day that story gained reality. "He did it! Dillinger robbed the State Bank." I heard that while I was in school. Now it's one thing to read about him in the newspaper and another to have him shooting off his guns in your home town. But I was feeling very safe: Dillinger may have been tough but he wouldn't rob a *school.*

The report was that he held up that bank again because, "It was so easy the first time." What Dillinger didn't know was that, after the first robbery, the local police vowed: "Not again." We heard they had armed themselves with a Tommy gun. A Thompson submachine gun. We could see the new police pursuit car for sure. It was a big, black Buick with a one-inch bullet proof windshield, complete with gun port. For the Tommy gun I assumed.

After the first report of the hold-up, the town lay quiet in suspense. Was Dillinger still there? A robber on the loose turned the place into a potential shooting gallery. We looked out the school windows and the streets were empty. None of the town's male citizenry made a move to fight off crime. That's what they had hired the police for.

Would the cops in our town track down John Dillinger before he made his getaway? The question buzzed through my school. Our town would be famous. Better than getting hit by a zeppelin.

I wasn't to find out till they let us out of school, Dillinger's escapade apparently ended. I ran home as fast as I could. "Did they find him?" I asked, gasping for air.

"Oh, yes," my father replied. "They set up the police car across the road."

"What did Dillinger do?" I inquired eagerly.

"He just drove around it," my father said quietly. Then he added. "But the chief of police was ready for him. Stood in the rest of the road, blocking it."

"Really?"

"Yes."

"Then what did Dillinger do?" I had visions of our police chief bringing this hombre to justice. Our chief.

"Ran him down. Knocked the chief on his can," my father said. He went on to explain that the chief had escaped with only bruises and a broken arm. "Damn fool," my father seemed to mutter under his breath.

Was it really Dillinger? Everyone in town said so. However, years later a check in the morgue of the local paper revealed only: "Thugs Hold Up State Bank."

So maybe John Milliner never came there after all. But it surely was a better headline in the newspaper than say, "County's Crop Eaten by Grasshoppers."

11

The Reel Lawn Mower

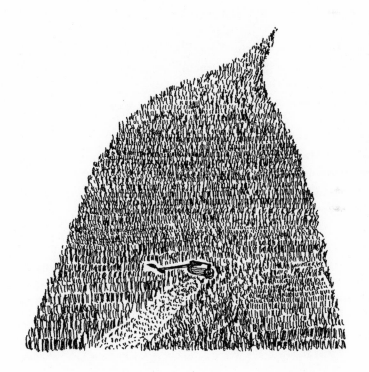

We spent the night in some trailer park near El Paso. The name of it escapes me; I think it was something like "Rotten Ralph's RV Roundup." At least we'd left Bide-a-Wee country. Though these names do join a lexicon of poor taste such as the bar I had spotted once in Des Moines, Iowa: the "Ran Da Voo." As a matter of fact all these were a cut above our next stop: "The Kozy Komfort Kamper Kort." Which leads me to wonder: Why can't people leave good names alone? Use "Plaza Court." Or "The Willows." Or "Lakeside Motel"—which probably is four blocks from the lake, anyway.

Even for a time—before the interstate highways and large chains knocked them out—it got to the point where the landscape was dotted with couple-owned motels that incorporated the participants' first names. "Wilmar" comes to mind. That perhaps led to "Claraphil Court." Barbara and I conjectured that if we were to ever open a similar establishment we could envision it as, simply, the "Barf Motel."

As we lurched out of El Paso, Barbara went to the back to put our newly purchased groceries in the refrigerator and other appropriate niches. The Chinook rides best in the cab. From there on to the rear end the amount of jouncing, jiggling and just plain pounding can be charted as a geometric progression. Add to that the sway—and the road's own ruts, ridges and rambling—and putting away groceries on the move was like trying to play pinball in a freight car moving at sixty-five miles an hour.

"How's it going?" I shouted. That was just a gesture. The noise covered my voice; she couldn't hear a word.

I looked over at the passenger seat—where Felix had started the day's journey. Not there. He'd fled the seat for the safety of the transmission hump. Only today he'd decided he wouldn't even face forward. He had pushed his face to the rise behind the cab. That way he'd look at nothing, just stare at the carpet, body hunched up behind. Suffering. I wondered if every night when we stopped, Felix conjectured that the ordeal was over. So every morning when we rolled down the road again—he felt, surely, that we were on an endless trip. There was no way to tell him that the trip would end. Wouldn't it?

Barbara slid into the seat, being careful not to step on the cat.

Felix might feel insecure but as we traveled on it was not a feeling he would pick up from Barbara and me. Pulling up to move always generates a certain amount of risk but you might say that neither of us had anything to anchor us for the remainder of our lives in the place we'd just left. Our tenure in southern Illinois was now part of the past.

Certainly houses weren't holding us back. Owning a house can be a tremendous asset. It's probably the best way Americans have of building an accumulation of capital. A very sound, secure way of life. I remember a friend of mine, Harry. A "program shift" at a western university had propelled Harry into freelance photography—out the office door and onto the street. "At least my house is all paid for," he said, sighing in reflection of years of skimping to make heavy house payments. Only a couple of years later his *widow's* house was just that—all paid for.

Most people enjoy having houses. At least I suppose they do. They put considerable time and money into them. Of course otherwise the damn things would fall down. I could recall all that fun. Scraping paint from peeling window frames. Watching the chimney bricks bounce down the roof. Cleaning leaves—nine hundred tons of leaves—out of roof gutters.

Water damage. That's great too. I'd never known river floods. Just a lake. Inside a house. It had formed in the upstairs from a toilet tank that suddenly cracked open. I became aware that something was amiss when a stream of water gushed forth from the light fixture in the living room ceiling. The lake, I then discovered after pounding up the stairs, was only one inch deep. But it ran the length and width of the whole house.

I was very busy for the next few hours.

Then there was lawn mowing. I know; many people derive great satisfaction, even therapy, from their lawns and gardens. Barbara's father, on his retirement, had successfully transferred his job time energy for an oil company directly into his gladiolas.

Even for me lawn mowing used to carry a certain nostalgic charm. As a child, growing up, I would often slowly awaken to the whirring clicks as the revolving blades of reel lawnmowers sliced through the grass, back and forth, heralding the start of another summer day on our quiet Iowa street. First the robins cheeping, then the first tick—tick, tick, tick-tick as the mower moved into motion.

In practically no time at all, I then learned what made one of those lawn mowers go. The propelling force. Me. I also learned why Iowans mowed their lawns fairly early in the day; later on it was just too, too hot.

It wasn't just the simple act of mowing either. Proper Midwest Lawn Care dictated that you—I, in this case—attach a metal and canvas grass catcher behind the hand mower. At certain times, either when the basket was full or a break was needed, you took the clippings and piled them up somewhere. If you were truly smart you turned them into a compost heap, which later could be put on the lawn—to make it grow even higher and faster, of course. Finally, according to the

Well-Manicured Lawn Code, the edges at sidewalks and driveways and curbs were trimmed. Not by one of these whirring string things they have nowadays. By a little hand cutter. In your little hand. On your knees.

As long as you were down there too, you could scrunch on over to the freshly cut turf and dig out the dandelions. All four thousand one hundred and sixty seven of them.

So I knew about houses and gardens.

Somehow along the way, Barbara had left the last house she'd shared with her former husband in the care of the former husband she'd shared it with. And at another juncture, quite separate, a piece of paper had informed me that my wife, former wife at that point, was taking half of everything I had. Except the house. She took all of that.

That meant neither of us had to worry about those things any more.

Barbara looked up from the New Mexico map she was studying. We'd spent the first part of the day exploring El Paso and were now on U.S. 54, north to Alamogordo. The western face of the Sacramento Mountains, paralleling our route and warmed by the mauve afternoon light, escorted us benignly.

"There's a place called Oliver Lee State Park along here that looks interesting," Barbara announced. "We could stop and walk up to a mountain spring."

"As long as I don't have to trim along the sidewalks and pull the dandelions," I said.

"What?" she asked, puzzled.

"Oh," I responded, "I must have been reliving some treasured memories of my childhood."

12

Kozy Komfort

The Kozy Komfort Kamper Kort in Alamogordo proved to be just that. Kozy. Jowl by cheek. But we weren't interested in space, just electricity. I still hadn't figured out why the furnace didn't work at night but at this moment it didn't matter. For backup, in just such emergencies, we had carefully placed among our load of equipment—an electric blanket. For this night then we plugged the RV in to good old AC power and fired up the blanket.

Emerging from the depths of the same the next morning, I made a few tests to be sure my vocal cords functioned. Then I allowed as how, "I was really too hot last night. This blanket's gone crazy."

"Really," Barbara murmured, her head still below covers. "I was way too cold."

"Oh," I said cautiously. "Different body temperatures probably."

"No," Barbara came back, surfacing. "Different controls. We have them switched."

I looked. Sure enough. "I got so hot I kept turning mine down, of course."

"Of course," Barbara echoed. "Whereupon I would turn mine up."

"At least you had Felix," I added.

"You're the electrical genius," Barbara muttered aloud. "No wonder the electric fan sucks air rather than blowing it."

"You just have to turn it around and sit on the other side," I replied. "Simple."

"Well then, Mr. Edison, how about putting together some morning tea?"

The Chinook is cozy. So much so that the stove was right by my head. With the teakettle filled I could do everything from my side of the bed—without having to expose myself to the frosty morning air.

As we sipped our Earl Grey we pondered the day ahead. For the first time it seemed like we weren't just "on the go." We were settling into camping, looking around, and discovering each day's treasures.

"First, we'll have to have a doughnut," Barbara said, to open the topic of breakfast. We had found an Alamogordo outlet of a chain with good doughnuts. However with our dietary concerns, doughnuts had achieved the status a special taste treat. We reserved these jewels for road trips and even then ate only three or four of the holy specimens a year.

"These are all right," I mumbled with a full mouth, "but not as good as the ones in Manistique," I put in.

"No, couldn't be," Barbara added. This referred to some benchmark in doughnutry we had found in a supermarket deli in Manistique, Michigan. From that time on, we compared all doughnuts to the succulent, home-style, crunchy exterior and soft, mouth-watering interior of the Manistique marvels.

"That reminds me," I said. "Among things I will miss about the Midwest are smoked Great Lakes whitefish. That day we went whitefish crazy near Charlevoix. Smoked whitefish for breakfast and lunch."

"Then you steamed another one in the cooker for dinner," Barbara added.

"You bet," I said.

"You Iowans say that a lot."

"What?"

"'You bet.' You say that after all sorts of comments."

"I think Missourians say, 'You bet' too," I put in.

"What about people in Minnesota?" Barbara asked.

"Well, if they live near the Canadian border I suppose they say, 'You bet, eh.'"

Barbara paused to reflect, "I suppose another thing I'm going to miss about living there are those big Midwest thunderstorms. Terrifying at times. Tornadoes at times. But those boiling mountains of air—with the lightning behind one layer of clouds, outlining another. And the sounds of thunder booming down on hundreds of square miles of prairie. There's nothing quite like them."

"I remember my friend Don, after he came to Illinois from living in California, used to take a chair in the backyard just to sit and watch an approaching thunderstorm," I said. "Sometimes for hours."

"Come to think of it," I said, "when I was a child, thunderstorms were simply a dramatic part of living in Iowa. My room was under the eaves and I remember waking to hear the wind rise, the limbs start to creak in the big poplar tree by the house; then there'd be the first splat, splat, splat of large drops, usually followed by a rush of windblown rain. Maybe it was just the odor from freshly washed leaves but you could smell the rain. Then came the lightning, the great claps of thunder. Whatever fear this may have brought to me was then quenched by a feeling of great security—when a parent would arrive to close down the windows against the storm. Then I felt safe," I concluded.

"You didn't know much about tornadoes then, apparently," Barbara added laughing.

"We knew. It's just that there were no "Tornado Watches" then so there was less time to worry about being blown away."

"True."

"Remembering my childhood bedroom takes me back to winter mornings," I said. "Usually once a winter there would be that moment when I'd come to wakefulness and realize the world around me was a quieter place. Sounds were almost nonexistent—or, if there—muffled. It would be then that I would realize that the night had brought the first snowfall. The blanket of white covered the "liveness" of sound transmission. All was muted. Then, breaking the quiet, would come the scrape, scrape, scrape of a snow shovel. The spell was cracked; the magic had seeped out. I had to get up."

"Obviously you won't miss the rest of the charms of snow," Barbara added. "What do you think you'll miss most about the Midwest?"

I didn't have to pause to think. I knew: "The Mississippi River."

Then I did pause to reflect: "As a kid I used to sit on the banks of the Skunk River in Iowa. I knew that the water I was watching move past me was going on to the Mississippi."

It was on that riverbank that I first dreamed the dreams of voyages to other places. Later I found excitement in the river towns. 'Front Street' or 'River Street' would invariably lure me into the old waterfronts—to wonder if Samuel Clemens or Richard Bissell had walked those bricks—and to watch the modern tows rumbling past the banks and levees. Clinton and Keokuk. Grafton and Grand Tower. Hannibal and Cairo. New Madrid and Natchez.

Does any Midwesterner—that dull, prosaic but not-to-be-denied term of birthplace—ever divorce himself from the great rivers of that region. I couldn't. The Mississippi flowed right through the middle of my life—just as it did through the country. My escapades, my dalliances, my loves, so often took their settings on the edges of those sepia waters. Once, in a moment of my miscalculation, that river could have taken my life—as it had the lives of others who forgot, for one fatal instant, its power.

Then too it gave me a renewal of life. A rekindling of spirit. At low times—divorce, death—I found I could go to the banks of the river—and the silent rush of its waters would tell me to move on: find something else in my mind's terrain. Move on and try to leave grief behind—where it belonged—in the caverns of the past.

"Yes. I'll miss that," I said.

"You're really carried away this morning," Barbara responded.

"I could sing you a bit of 'Ol Man River,'" I continued, practicing my "O, O, O's."

"I'd rather have a doughnut, if you don't mind," she said.

13

Land of Numina

In the distance it spread across the landscape as a large, white lake. Like a mirage. It was the White Sands National Monument of New Mexico. As we headed southwest from Alamogordo, the cotton-ball cumulus clouds accented the intense blue sky but didn't block the clean pure light from a brilliant sun. We drew closer. The dunes then revealed their individual shapes, opening magic vistas in this "sea."

"Actually," I explained to Barbara, "this shouldn't be called White Sands at all, because it isn't sand."

"Not sand?"

"Sand is particles ground up out of rock. This is gypsum. It comes instead from a drying process—over at Lake Lucero here. Since it's gypsum, those particles make their own special kinds of dunes as the wind moves them."

"That explains why this place is special," Barbara said. "But how do you know so much about it?"

"I just know. Smart."

"Smart? Smartass."

"I even know the first law of thermodynamics," I announced.

"You think you're pretty hot stuff."

"No, that's the second law of thermodynamics. "It says…""

Barbara started cuffing my upper head. "Spare me."

She finally stopped and I said, "Actually I knew about White Sands because I read about it when I was filming here."

I had been intrigued by this area since my first visit in 1959. Subsequently I made a 16 mm film which made visual comparisons of the shapes of the dunes and the mountains and the flora to the contours and patterns of a woman's body. I called the five-minute film *Numina* which means "spirits." I had always thought of the White sands—and all of New Mexico, for that matter—as a place of spirits. Sometimes I suppose I think of a woman's body that way too. I don't know. Anyway I tried to make the film a celebration of forms and shapes and textures.

The forms around us now were the many sparkling dunes. As we wound our way down the road, the textures of sparse vegetation gave out, abandoning the scene completely to the gypsum dunes.

There was nothing but white all around.

It was a relief to be here in the winter—jacket weather. My filming had all been done in July. The sun then can really fry your brains.

"This will give us a chance to give Felix an airing," Barbara said. We were afraid to walk him in motor home parks; too many cubbyholes for him to dart into.

We carefully inserted him into his harness and leash. Felix made a beeline to the first dune. The breeze ruffled his long fur coat. He checked the terrain, sniffed the air, and marched on up the dune. Then he did what I suppose any cat—faced with the largest white sandbox in, maybe, the world—would do. He dug a hole. Sat over it for a few moments of concentration. Then discreetly covered it all over.

Cats may be Republicans, they may be Democrats—but universally they are, without exception—pragmatists.

A sandbox is a sandbox.

I'd like to report that I then did the correct thing; dug it up and disposed of it properly. I'd like to report that. I really would.

Barbara and Felix then carried on with their outing while I took a few pictures. When we all arrived back at the Chinook Felix squatted down in a lump on the white ground. Obviously he didn't want to leave. Maybe the spirits had invaded his small body.

Not wishing to enter into a debate on this though we hoisted him aboard.

We left White Sands on U.S. 70/80. The highway started climbing—up past the craggy, exciting shapes of the Organ Mountains.

As people have known for centuries, New Mexico can seduce you with its magic.

"I could live here," Barbara said. "What a special place."

Climbing through the pass we started down, descending into Las Cruces. We began looking for La Mesilla State Monument.

"The map shows that it's somewhere south of town," I said. I was navigating.

"Which exit should I take?" Barbara asked.

I studied the map. "Take the next one," I said positively.

"I don't see any signs," she confirmed as we approached the ramp.

"Go on to the next exit then. If we don't see any signs there we'll get off anyway."

We moved on to the next exit.

"No sign here either."

As we went off the highway I resumed looking at the map.

"There's some sign about Mesilla at the intersection ahead," I continued. "Go down this road. South."

No more signs.

We went down that road—south—for quite a while.

"Why don't we pull in what is commonly called a filling station and ask?" Barbara wondered.

"This map's not very detailed," I offered as some sort of explanation.

"I know the map's not very helpful," Barbara said. "I'm not criticizing your navigation."

We continued down the road.

She spoke up again: "Why don't we just ask someone?"

I presume the tradition that men won't stop a vehicle and ask simple directions goes well back into history. I can even hear Mrs. Columbus saying, "So pull over, Chris baby. Just ask. Pull in at the next island. *They* can tell you where the East Indies are."

I swallowed hard. "The people in filling stations don't usually know."

"Well," Barbara came back, "down *this* far they may not. We're almost in Mexico!"

"Okay, turn around. We'll head back."

"And find a filling station," I mumbled. I know when I'm licked. But we'd only been wandering around for maybe forty-five minutes. "It would have helped to have a better map," I concluded.

But Barbara wasn't listening. She had lowered the window as we entered the next gas station and was listening carefully to the explicit instructions.

We turned. Westward. She commented, "It's right over there a few blocks."

"I knew we were close," I replied.

We explored the adobe buildings of Mesilla. It was once the largest town in the territory, later a center for the western campaigns of the Confederate Army. Now it was quiet and subdued, all that life and turmoil moved elsewhere. A plaque announced that Billy the Kid had been put on trial here. And sentenced to be hanged.

I guess Billy hadn't needed a roadmap to find the place.

14

Cats Through the Ages

Leaving Las Cruces, we headed for New Mexico's Rock Hound State Park. It was not that we are rock hounds—but whenever we can we like to stay in state parks. Often they convey certain essential flavors of their state. Prairie Rose State Park, the name truly says it all, in Iowa comes to mind. A peaceful place, its open areas a sea of long grasses. There pheasants scurried about, trying to lead us the opposite direction from their young. Or Valley of the Rogue State Park in Oregon, where the tumbling waters of the Rogue River sing the sound of a lullaby at night. Or Galveston Island State Park in Texas with the waters of the Gulf to wake you at morning light.

Settled in at Rock Hound—and plugged in electrically against the predicted cold—we set about feeding. First Felix. He observes regularity like a digital watch. Once fed, he usually settled in next to one of us, getting his body as close as possible. He seemed to be saying: "I've put up with all this bouncing around all day. Now I want some companionship, a soothing spot."

I realize cats like to get on, around, by people because people are warm. Just that. Warm. Yet at times I wonder if it doesn't go beyond that. In a household environment, Felix will go weeks without stepping into the bedroom. Yet if Barbara and I go away for one overnight—and up to that time he's been sleeping and eating out of doors regularly—when we return he camps by our bed for two or three nights. Like he's afraid we'll desert him again. Sometimes then when he's really testing, he'll come lie on the bed next to me in the morning: "You're not going to leave me all alone today are you?"

I'm sure there was speculation about the communication between man and animal even before history. There seems no doubt that something gets exchanged. I recall my friend Dick and his dog Easy. Dick would drive away from home untold numbers of times, even with luggage for short trips, with hardly a nod from Easy. But the day Dick was to drive away for a four-month sabbatical leave, Easy knew something different was happening. So much so that he physically blocked Dick from getting in the car. Then finally having lost that battle, Easy sat in the driveway in front of the car refusing to budge. "Over my dead body." Needless to say, Easy was finally moved before Dick's sabbatical ran out. But it does make you wonder what Easy knew that told him this was different. Some change in Dick's body chemistry that Easy's wonderfully sensitive nose picked up? Maybe someday we'll know more about how we communicate with animals.

Maybe someday we'll even figure out how to communicate with each other.

Apparently cats evolved to their present form fairly early in the cycle of things. But their problem was that nobody cared; nobody wanted cats.

You can just see this couple sitting in their cave. Mr. and Mrs. Uggh. And of course their son, Mug Uggh.

Mr. Uggh speaks: "What is the furry thing you brought home, Mug?"

"Don't know, pa."

"I hear," Mrs. Uggh interjected, "that they are called 'cats'."

"What good are they?"

"I have no idea."

"Can we eat them?" Mr. Uggh proposed.

"They're kind of scrawny," Mrs. U. replied.

"Will they help me hunt?"

"They seem to hunt on their own," Mug put in.

Mr. Uggh pondered all this. Then he announced, "Throw that cat out of here. Next time, Mug, bring home something more useful like those, those—what are they?"

"Dogs," Mrs. Uggh replied. "Dogs."

So cats had to exist on their own for centuries. Which they did quite well—and still do. A house cat can usually survive solo if it has to. For dogs it's tougher—unless they form packs. Which, since they are social, is also likely a reason they easily form bonds with humans.

Cats were out there in the cold until maybe around maybe 15 hundred B.C.. Then something happened in ancient Egypt. Old man Pharaoh was complaining at length: "Isn't enough I have trouble with the Israelites? Now something is munching up all our grain. What the hell is going on? I ask."

"Now, now," the Queen put in. "There must be something can be done. At least about the grain. It's those rats, Pharaoh baby. Gotta get those rats."

"I tried, Queenie," he came back. "I tried that one animal."

"You mean those four-legged things with tails that wag?"

"Yeah, dogs. They don't work worth a damn." He sat pondering for a long time. "I'm thinking of shipping the whole lot of them off to the Red Sea."

"The dogs?"

"No, the Israelites," he responded. "I think we ought to just let the dogs go. There must be something better."

"Dear," said the Queen—she always called old Pharaoh that when she wanted to propose something—"while barging on the Nile the other day I ran into some peddler guy selling some new creature. He said it was rat-oriented."

"What's it called?" inquired his royal highness.

"He calls them 'cats'."

"Get a dozen, baby. We'll give them a try. If they work out," the Pharaoh went on, "we'll make them gods and worship them."

The rest, as we know, is history. The Egyptians ended up calling their cat-god, oh so phonetically, "Myeo." When a cat died, they mourned as if for a person. They even mummified them and gave them mummified mice for the afterworld.

Cats did pretty well then for a while. Greeks liked them. It's even rumored that Archimedes didn't discover the principle of weight and displacement while bathing himself. He was bathing his family cat, "Eureka."

Romans liked cats—as anyone treading the streets of Rome to this day can testify.

The Welsh enacted laws protecting cats.

Then came the Dark Ages and everything went to Hell, literally and figuratively. Growing out of a superstitious fear of feline powers, Christianity became the only religion in the world to torture and kill cats. Of course the religious leaders then did that to people too so we shouldn't be surprised. Maybe if those leaders had paid more attention to rats than to cats we wouldn't have had the Plague.

Religious burning of live cats stopped around the time of increased settlement in the New World. It might even be speculated that cats came to America around 1750 in pursuit of religious freedom. But that's pushing it a bit.

Actually they loaded ships up with cats and brought them to the thirteen colonies for the same reason they loaded ships with slaves: To Help With the Crops. Pennsylvania farmers were having a lot of trouble with rats. Even the hex signs on the barns weren't doing any good. So they simply imported cats.

Now there are an estimated 30 million of them walking around the United States.

That freedom to roam resulted in attempts to counter it. Vetoing one such myopic piece of legislative zeal led to this message by the statesman Adlai Stevenson, then governor of the Land of Lincoln: "I cannot agree that it should be the declared public policy of Illinois that a cat visiting a neighbor's yard or crossing the highway is a public nuisance. It is in the nature of cats to do a certain amount of roaming—to escort a cat abroad on a leash is against the nature of the owner. Moreover cats perform useful service, particularly in the rural areas. The problem of the cat vs. the bird is as old as time. If we attempt to resolve it by legislation, who knows but what we may be called upon to take sides as well in the age-old problems of dog vs. cat, bird vs. bird or even bird vs. worm. In my opinion, the State of Illinois and its local governing bodies already have enough to do without trying to control feline delinquency."

Of course it should be pointed out that in the relationship between people and cats there is always the matter of superiority. It's simple. Cats know they are superior. But they're tolerant. They'll put up with a certain amount of cootchy talk, overdone petting and even an accidentally stepped-on tail if they can maintain control of the household.

Sometimes, though, cats do need that extra touch of help from us—just to get through the day.

That night in Rock Hound we were ready for our after dinner tea. I had put the kettle on the gas burner and resumed reading, waiting for the summons of whistling steam. Something though passed my nostrils. "Do you smell anything, Barbara?"

"No, not particularly. But then I'm a little stuffed up."

"Hmm. I'd swear I smelled something odd." Smelling something odd in a motor home—with gasoline, propane and whatever other combustibles surrounding you—is a distinctly nerve-tingling experience. I looked around quickly and didn't see anything too unusual. Felix had taken up a sitting spot on the rear counter next to the stove. But he wouldn't get in the fire.

"Now I smell something," Barbara said, also looking around. "It smells like…"

"Like hair," I said louder. "Felix?" I said as if to question him. Felix looked up—as he always does when addressed by name. But no look of distress crossed his face.

Then I saw it. From behind Felix a wisp of smoke was rising into the air. Barbara and I lunged for him at the same time.

"Felix, you're on fire," I shouted.

I carried him away from the burner while Barbara beat on his smoldering tail with her hands.

Somehow the picture of Felix frantically flying around the perimeter walls of the Chinook, chased by a smoking tail, was not one I cared to dwell on.

Felix did not understand what the fuss was all about. Apparently the long hairs had started to go but his nerve endings hadn't yet detected the impending problem.

Something must have registered with Felix though. He never sat that close to the stove again.

Barbara took him in her arms to hold him and smooth down the fur of his body against any imagined ills. Then she lightly ran her hand down his tail to cover the singed spot.

Felix looked up at me as if to say: "That's all right, buster. Doc Floogle told me there'd be days like this."

"But don't let it happen again."

15

Kitty and Me

My history with cats goes back to childhood. When I was seven years old my mother asked me if I'd like a cat—as a birthday present. Since it was winter, I perceived this as some sort of ploy by my parents to get out of buying me a new sled. It looked like I would have to use my brother's sled *forever*. It was big and heavy; I think it weighed about sixty pounds and he probably had used it until he finished college and got married. "But it's a heavy duty sled," my parents would point out. "*Heavy* duty sled." I would mumble in response. At least they'd sold his saxophone. I wouldn't have to cope with that.

So sometime before my seventh year passed into history, my mother, my aunt and I drove forth into the Iowa countryside in search of a cat. Somehow we found a farm with kittens—not that that's very hard to do in a rural state. My Aunt Ruth was in charge of the expedition. She'd had cats around her all her life, from girlhood on. She was my cat mentor.

With no hesitation my aunt suggested I select a small gray bit of fur, one with a white dot in the middle of its chest and black rings around its tail. Holding the creature on my lap on the trip home, I queried Aunt Ruth about the various criteria in her selection process. Her answer was succinct: "I picked the one that didn't meow much." During the rest of that cat's life with me I often acknowledged the wisdom of her choice. The cat would speak when necessary—but not much beyond that.

Felix was even quieter. Which made me appreciate him all the more. Otherwise he might still be back scrounging up a living in southern Illinois.

Reading up on cats, I see that experts say that the creatures actually don't mind water. I'm not so sure about that. I do know that my childhood cat, however, had a fondness for the family bathtub. But empty. Dry. The tub was the old four-legged clawfoot type. Yet ours stood on only three legs. Someone had never gotten the right front one into place. We never told anyone we had a three-legged bathtub. It's not something you want to brag about or even explain. A family secret. But not as big as the one about an uncle who was given a round-trip ticket to go all the way to California to represent the whole family at a funeral. But he took it as a one-way journey from wife and child. He vanished.

Anyway, our old tub didn't teeter; it just sat there in our tiny second-floor bathroom. Where it sat though was quite marvelous; it was directly over a hot air register. That tub was always warm in winter, wet or dry. A great retreat for a cat's daytime slumbers. The cat would hop on a clothes hamper at one end of the tub, check out the tub's liquid condition and, finding it dry, hop down in. The cat even got to the point where it would pull the bathmat down from one side of the tub for a softer bed.

Gradually, though, our cat's natural caution was overcome by overconfidence. She stopped checking things out from the hamper. She'd just jump straight up from the floor, over the edge, into the tub.

The inevitable of course was coming. One day I had drawn a morning bath and was downstairs getting my daily fix of Ovaltine. I heard a distinct splash. Fearing something disastrous might have happened, I ran for the stairs. Coming down them marched my cat, dripping wet, ears pulled back and scowling with rage. I've seen mad cats but that was the maddest ever. She didn't even pause to lick off the offending water, just lit out for the basement—to hide her shame I guess.

For a long time she never went near that tub.

She *may* have tolerated water before then but from that day forward, that cat greeted wetness with unmistakable disdain.

By now you've noticed that I'm not designating my childhood cat by name. It's just that I never got a suitable one picked out. When it was still a kitten, my mother urged me to name it. I suggested calling it "American Flyer" for the sled I wasn't getting, but that wasn't even greeted by my parents for the humor I was trying, albeit sarcastically, to convey.

As for names, I had always wanted, instead of my given name, to be called "Buck." But "Buck" wouldn't do for a female cat, even a spayed one. For a while I considered naming the cat for one of the girls I fancied in third grade: Mary Frances. Or fourth grade: Mary Jean. Or fifth: Mary Ellen. By sixth grade I'd run out of "Mary's"—and the cat was too old to respond to any name but "Kitty."

Come to think of it, of all the women I've been involved with in my life there's never been a Mary. That connection must have been worn out before puberty took its toll. Kitty, though, was Kitty until the day she died, at age fourteen. 1 was away in the Army Air Force. My mother brought me the news when she came to visit me at Lowry Field, Colorado. I was saddened but I was young, with only my father's death as a reference point. However, my mother said she grieved as if for a person. Maybe it was because the cat's life measured a span of time in her life that was filled with larger tragedies. Those time spans become a coordinate—on the graph of the attrition that life holds for us.

With Kitty's demise I didn't have much to do with cats for a long, long, time. Not that my choice had anything to do with my feelings in the matter—just a lot of moving around precluded having a pet.

At one point a few cats had shown up in a farmhouse where I lived. They were fun—and they belonged next door. Except one did come in to our house to have her kittens. I had a chance to finally observe all that natural phenomenon. At age fifty-six part of my sex education was at last complete. Subsequently though, I did pass up the opportunity to keep any—or all—five kittens.

Traces of my life with my first gray cat emerge, even now, in family snapshots. I found some the other day. In them I'm holding the cat in various poses. Gradually the photos show me getting larger—and, of course, the cat stays the same. One of the early pictures shows me at, maybe, eight. I am standing by the back screen door. The cat is under one arm, the other arm supporting her rear legs. Some people just let cats dangle. I always thought I wouldn't like to dangle my rear legs if someone picked me up—so I do the same for cats. I have no idea if the cats care or not.

Mostly they just want *down*. In the snapshot, my cat is looking about for a suitable escape. I'm smiling, pleased to have her. I was looking at that photo recently—some half a century after it was clicked into being in the family Kodak box camera. I turned the print over and discovered that my now long-dead mother had penned something on the back. It said: "Not much to look at but pleasant to have around." God! Did she mean me? Or the cat? Now I'll never know. You did mean the cat—Didn't you, mom?

16

Highway Robbery at Cactus Jack's

As we rolled westward from Deming, New Mexico, on Interstate 10, I began to notice something in the air.

"What are those funny white things blowing around us?" I asked grimly.

"I hate to say it," Barbara replied, "but I think it is called snow. S-N-O-W."

"Ye gods!" I exclaimed. "That's absurd. This is southern New Mexico. I picked this route to avoid such stuff. It's a conspiracy!"

"Now, now," Barbara said, trying to calm me down.

"I mean the only more southern route to go to California would be to go through the Panama Canal!"

Being relatively sure it was not snowing in San Diego, I turned the direction finder in my brain to that frequency and resolutely plowed on. In more ways than one; the snow was piling up. People were pulling off the road to do whatever people do when they pull off the road in snow or rain. Wait for it to get better I guess. Being raised in Iowa, I generally viewed such a gesture as an exercise in futility. In Iowa weather, waiting for it to get better might mean waiting until the following week.

I wasn't even slowing down. I figured the snow storm was moving to the East—so if we went to the West *far enough* we'd leave it behind.

This hope was finally realized somewhere shy of Tucson. Following the storm's visit, however, the mountains all around us were white with snow. Though I'd driven this route before, the new cover on the hills and ridges dramatized the peaks in a fresh way. They looked more like the Bighorn Mountains of Wyoming than the Galiuro Mountains of Arizona. It was exhilarating in its rarity.

However, if I registered surprise at finding snow here, it was nothing compared to the reaction of Tucsononians. They had actually seen it on their streets that day. It was as incredible as meeting a tongue-tied car salesman.

The sun came up over the mountains east of Tucson the next morning—thereby restoring the faith of its citizens in Nature's ways.

We took that as a cue to explore the city.

In one Indian shop I happened to notice a black velvet wall hanging. It was a large portrait of John Wayne. That struck me as a little odd—for the people who, on the screen, had been blown away by so many of the Duke's Hollywood bullets. Then I noticed that the Wayne face beneath the gray Stetson was colored a light but unmistakable—green. A bilious green you might say. The Apache's revenge.

We climbed out of Tucson to visit another favorite spot in my museum collection—the Arizona-Sonora Desert Museum. They say that they have one of the most magnificent saguaro forests in the world. We agreed so wholeheartedly that we surrendered to the beauty of the tall cactus fingers all around us. We stayed then to camp that night in nearby Tucson Mountain Park.

In this park the coyotes lope right through the camp sites looking for food. The next morning I pointed one out to Felix. "See, Felix, he's here looking for his first meal of the day."

Felix barely gave the creature a passing glance.

"Namely," I continued, "you."

Felix turned away, pretending to ignore Señor Coyoté and the whole situation.

I hardly need add that this was one place we didn't chance taking Felix walking on his leash. I could easily envision our coyote visitor sitting down to a tasty treat of filet of Felix.

From the Mountain Park we then headed the Chinook west and south, to a destination we had picked yesterday at the Desert Museum. There an identification plate next to an organ pipe cactus pointed out that it grew naturally in the United States in only one place—Organ Pipe Cactus National Monument. This park lies in the very southernmost part of Arizona, on the Mexican border. Naturally we had to investigate a place like that.

As we trundled down Arizona highway 86, the crosswind slowed our progress. You may recall that I once mentioned our highway speed as fifty-five. It has little to do with compliance with the laws of the land. It just happens that that is about as fast as the Chinook will go. Headwinds and crosswinds impose limits, though the shape of the vehicle is aerodynamic enough to keep the rig nicely nailed down to the roadway.

A tailwind though, with the vehicle's large flat rear surface, is something special. One time in South Dakota the wind was directly at our back. That in itself is unusual; almost always in the Dakotas you buck a fierce headwind. And, I might add, it does not matter which direction you head. In South Dakota—and, North Dakota as well—the wind seems to be universally *against* you. This time though, a freak occurrence had taken hold and we were sailing down the highway with the wind at our back. At seventy-five miles an hour. In the Chinook it felt like 150. Of course it was short-lived. Up the line we had to make a right angle turn to go north. However, the wind didn't. It then pushed hard against our side the rest of the way to Minnesota.

This time in Arizona the wind wasn't quite so severe. We made Organ Pipe at nightfall.

It was the next day, in the middle of all those cacti, that we learned Felix enjoyed walking amongst the spiny plants. His heavy fur let him get among them—to places we were fearful of going. He liked that.

He even tried it once without his leash. We were stopped for picture taking and I hesitated a moment too long in closing the front door.

Felix leaped free and bounded to the sand.

I laid my camera on the ground and, obeying *my* animal instincts, set off in pursuit.

Barbara stood by the Chinook shouting, "Don't chase him. Don't chase him! He'll just run faster!"

By then Felix was dodging through the cacti. A broken field run.

I was making an end sweep. I couldn't see letting him get farther away. No telling where he'd stop.

Felix twisted to the left.

Pounding in pursuit, I shouted, "Felix! Felix!"

He paid scant attention. Except to pick up his pace.

"Felix!" I screamed. "You're nothing but—but an *animal!*"

"Don't chase him!" Barbara shouted again as her contribution to the melee.

Felix darted right as I veered left. I nailed him—figuratively of course—between a saguaro and an organ pipe.

All the way back to the vehicle I lectured him. "Next time, Felix, Ranger Dan will arrest *you*. The park rules say you must be 'physically restrained at all times'!"

Felix didn't act one bit contrite. In fact I think he wanted to bite me. I smoothed his fur, trying to tell him about Gila monsters. He ignored me.

Reluctantly leaving the peace of the Sonora Desert, we headed for Yuma.

On the outskirts of Yuma we found a place to stop for the night. It was called something like "Cactus Jack's End of the Trail Mobile Home Haven." Space was cramped, so we had to park by Cactus Jack's front door. He arranged our electric hookup by sticking an extension cord out his bathroom window. The water connection came from Jack's water sprinkler system of course. What do you expect for $17.50? Things get tough out west. Jack also had a sign up by the park office announcing: "Prison Tours Arranged." I never figured out whether that meant tours of the old Arizona Territorial Prison—or was a message for those who might be considering stiffing old Jack for their camping fee.

We didn't try and find out.

The prison did turn out to be an intriguing place. Prisons do tend to be interesting—if you don't have to live in them.

Then back to the interstate.

Before Barbara knew it we were in California.

Our formal introduction and welcome to California lay down the line, of course. The official State Entrance Inspection Station. I knew that California is zealous in monitoring its borders for any invasions by bugs and other strange creatures. We were Ready, however. Our passports were up to date. Not only that—we had all Felix's papers in order: his rabies attestation, his flea records, his worm clearances, his birth certificate. House plants? We had carefully—and with some sadness—left our live plants with our friends Craig and Jan back in Illinois. We'd even consumed all the succulently flavored, home-grown citrus one Tucson RV park manager had bestowed upon us. We were *clean*.

We pulled into the motor home section of the station. "Welcome to California," said the young woman inspector.

I was going to do this by the book. No repeats of that border crossing from Canada to Maine when the U.S. Custom agents caught me in a lie about smuggling in lemon twists for my martinis. That time I thought I was surely facing five to ten in Leavenworth.

"Good morning," I replied cheerfully.

"May I take a look inside?" the inspector said pleasantly.

"Of course."

"Do you have any pets on board?"

"Yes, a cat. But we have all his records."

"It's not that," the young woman said. "It's just that be sure you hold it. Someone forgot to ask the other day and when we opened the door a cat got out. We had to run all over the freeway to catch the poor thing."

"You did get it back?" I asked for reassurance.

"Oh yes. But it was quite a merry chase for a while."

The inspection completed we rolled on.

Over a few more mountains, the Pacific Ocean. We looked forward to that. Felix seemed eager for new adventure too. He placed his paws on the dashboard and fixed his eyes on the road ahead.

17

You Can't Miss It

The true test of any relationship between a woman and a man is not decisions like: "Should we buy this house or the one across town that has a swimming pool?" Or: "Do you think we ought to put our life savings in 'The Little Gem Gold Mining Company'?" Or even: "Our offspring has been accepted by Harvard and Stanford but don't you think we ought to keep him close by at West Knothole State for a while until he matures?"

No. All these matters pale beside the crucial verification any coupling must face, the penultimate examination of their ability to endure as a twosome—being lost on a trip. Of course Barbara and I had already touched those little nerve endings while searching for Mesilla, New Mexico.

As we started our descent from the mountains above San Diego, we were about to find this situation was a tad more trying. We were even joking. "I thought you said it seldom rained here," I said.

"It doesn't rain all that much," Barbara replied.

"Then why can't I see more than 20 yards ahead?" I demanded, the windshield wipers whipping back and forth like a ball at Wimbledon.

"Surely it will let up."

Unfortunately no one heard.

The rain got worse.

"Let's pull off at the next town," I said. "What is it?"

Barbara studied the map. "I think we're approaching El Cajon."

"Welcome to El Cajon" the sign fairly shouted as we roared past, unable to switch lanes fast enough to exit.

I should point out here that our motor home—like most—is totally blind in the right rear corner. Like a panel truck. You check both wide-angle and flat-side mirrors first—to be sure no one is hidden on the right. Then you move over. Otherwise drivers of small cars are sometimes visibly undone.

"Try the next exit," Barbara said. "Maybe there's some place we can stay."

We moved carefully over and off the next ramp. I spotted a neon sign: "Happy Trails Parque and Campground." "Hey, there's a possibility," I said.

"Looks pretty expensive to me," Barbara said. "Let's see what's down the street."

Down the street flowed a river of water. The rain came in torrents. We floated, aquaplaned, plowed our way for a countless number of blocks. No further mobile home, trailer, RV, or any other kind of park showed up. We stopped to consider our options. We decided to go back to Happy Trails.

"How do we find it?" I asked since she was map-reader.

"Just get back on the interstate going east and then we'll turn around and come back."

"Okay."

We threaded our way through various turns and rolled up the ramp. Joining the traffic, I saw a sign flip by. "Where's a town called La Mesa?" I asked.

Barbara studied the map: "Wrong direction. We need to go the *other* way."

"The interstate must have decided to turn around," I said in a lame attempt at humor.

No one laughed.

Unbeknownst to us, the interstate had turned some while we were fording the local streets—which were also changing angles. Only in another direction.

"At least we know where we're headed. Even if it is the wrong way," Barbara commented.

"If you think that helps, try…" I mumbled incoherently.

"Whoops, here's an exit." I whipped us off and proceeded to make a series of turns in an attempt to put us back on the highway going the opposite direction.

"I don't see it," I announced.

"What?"

"The entrance to eastbound I-8."

"It's got to be here somewhere," Barbara said.

We drove on in the gloom.

Nothing.

"Don't be upset," Barbara said.

"What makes you think I'm upset?" I replied.

"Those foul words you keep shouting."

"Oh, that."

"It's just got to be here somewhere," Barbara commented.

Wrong. There was no eastbound ramp at that particular exit.

We drove for quite a while. The rain had lightened slightly. But to make up for that, darkness had now taken over.

We drove in silence.

Barbara, seeing some welcome lights through the wet, suggested we stop in a pleasant, plant bedecked restaurant across the way. Tea break. Time to calm down.

I agreed and started looking for a place to turn in. "Wait," I said, "There's no left turn here."

We continued on, searching for a way.

"What did He ever do to you?" Barbara asked.

"Who?"

"God. You keep yelling those things at him."

"Those," I replied in quieter tones, "are simply requests to Him to provide some eternal residence in the lower regions for the designers of this particular roadway."

We found a way to double back to the restaurant.

A spot of tea—as it generally always will—calmed us down. The rain had lightened. The people at the sprouts, wheat germ, and carrot cake restaurant were very pleasant.

We asked them directions to Happy Trails—or any RV park—but they had all just moved to California from Ohio and Wisconsin and didn't know where anything was. They did, most graciously, offer to let us spend the night in their parking lot. Unfortunately the combination of cold night air and the misbehaving furnace made us decline.

Back once more to the streets. Once more into the fray.

"Why don't I navigate and you drive?" I offered as a starter. "I'm pretty good at reading maps."

"Like back at La Mesilla," Barbara dryly commented.

"That was a very incomplete map." I replied.

"And this one?"

"Okay," I capitulated. "Let's give up on the interstate and we'll try and find Happy Trails by surface streets."

"And…" Barbara continued demandingly.

I knew when I was licked. I could give in gracefully. I tapped my fingers on the steering wheel. Fortunately it didn't break.

"And," I said, "we'll stop at a filling station to ask directions."

At least we were in a town where the streets were marked. We wouldn't have to cope with the missing street sign game so popular in some cities. On the alien streets of those places however they do atone for their lack of street-name signs—by being sure there are plenty of "One Way" signs—always in the opposite direction you desire to travel. As you may have noticed though, the citizens of Boston have no trouble with these impediments—they just merrily go the wrong way anyway.

In El Cajon we picked the next floodlit gas station and pulled in. I went in to get the information. "Do you know where Happy Trails RV Park is?"

The night manager weighed that a moment. "Hey, Fred," he called, "Ever hear of an RV place called Happy Trails?"

"Sure, Joe, that's the one that used to be the Sage and Sand."

"Oh, *that* place!" Joe replied. "It's easy. Which way you headed?"

I pointed.

"Go the opposite way down this street. You go eight lights. Or is it nine? Then you turn left. Go four lights. Maybe five. That'll bring you opposite a shopping center. With a McDonald's in it. There you turn right and…"

I was busy tabulating all this in my tired brain.

"No, no, no," broke in Fred, who had monitored the whole proceeding. "That's the *long* way. What you *ought* to do is cross the intersection here. Go east six blocks. Then south four blocks. There you'll find a Taco Bell on one corner and a gas station on the other. A Union 76 station."

"Naw," put in Joe. "It's a Chevron station."

"Anyway," continued Fred, "turn right there. Down three blocks on El Camino Real. In the middle of the next block you'll find an alley. That's Industrial Drive. Go four blocks…"

"Five, I think," interjected Joe.

"And you'll be there," concluded Fred. "You can't miss it."

I opened the door to the Chinook and sat down glumly.

"What did he say?," Barbara asked brightly.

"He said it's easy to find."

"He hasn't been riding with us the last two hours," she muttered grimly.

The rain was by then gushing down again. However, after finding only two McDonald's, three Union 76 gas stations and making two repeat trips through the parking lot of the same shopping center, we found before us the beckoning neon of Happy Trails Parque.

Somehow it didn't result in our breaking out in cheers.

I went in to the office to register. The manager was cordial. "Nasty night out. There were traffic problems all over the county."

"Really?"

"Yes. I hope you weren't out in it much. One thing about being here close to the highway—we're easy to find."

"Yes?"

"You can't miss it."

18

Felix On the Beach

What better way to celebrate our arrival at ocean's edge than an outdoor breakfast? We heard the surf calling us at our San Elijo campground site. A shirt-sleeve, sub-tropical, sun-filled morning in *December!* It was so alluring I didn't even stay in bed. We were trying some new Ceylon breakfast tea and I carried the cups immediately to the nearby picnic table. While Barbara collected the rest of breakfast I let Felix out to share the salubrious air. He sat down quietly by the back door of the Chinook, soaking it in.

"Do you think Felix needs his leash?" I called out.

"Does he seem to want to go away?" Barbara asked.

"No, he seems content to sit in the California sun."

On rare occasions, when Felix seemed disposed to sit rather than march off, we let him be free of the restraining harness and leash. We just kept an eye on him.

"It's ready," Barbara announced. I carried the plates of fresh orange slices and French toast on our cutting-board tray to the table. I sat down to arrange this and sip my tea, while awaiting Barbara. I looked back to check Felix.

"Did you put Felix back inside?" I asked, noting that he was no longer in sight.

"No," Barbara said, "I thought you had him."

I bounded to my feet and started frantically looking all around under the Chinook. Sometimes he took refuge there.

By then Barbara was out of the vehicle, scouting the camp site. "I don't see him."

"I don't see him either!" I responded. "He's gone, Barbara. He slipped away."

"Let's fan out and look," she offered.   .

We looked in the undergrowth. We looked in all the nearby campsites. We looked under other vehicles. No Felix.

Barbara kept calling, "Here, Felix. Here, Felix." He usually came when called. Not this time.

"Let's try his food bowl," I suggested. At home, when nothing else brought him trotting, the sound of dry food hitting the bowl worked almost one hundred per cent. Barbara poured a generous helping in the container. Then she rattled it. Nothing.

"Of course he's just eaten," she pointed out. "Let's go on up the road and look."

We searched the adjoining campsite area. Not a glimpse of Felix.

Beyond that the next area of campers yielded no more. Not in the bushes, not under picnic tables, not by trailers, nor up in trees.

"Let's try the beach," I said quietly. "He doesn't like beaches but—but I don't know where else to look."

"Yes," Barbara agreed softly.

The beach yielded nothing. But seeing dog tracks in the sand gave me an idea. "Hey, I'll look and see if I can see his prints around the Chinook. It's sandy there. At least we could see where he headed."

We headed back to the site, hopes up a little.

Some feline prints were in evidence close by but they disappeared in harder ground.

We sat down at the table. "I don't know where he could be, Barbara."

"I don't either."

"I thought I was watching him," I commented. "Damn."

We sat, saying nothing. Finally I just let it come out: "He's gone, Barbara. He's really gone."

"It's not your fault."

"I just looked away for an instant."

"You know how he is," Barbara said. "When he gets it in his mind to go, he goes."

"I shouldn't have given him the chance."

"You thought he was all right."

"I was wrong," I offered.

"It's just not your fault," Barbara repeated.

We both sat in silence again, sipping our cold—now bitter—tea.

Finally Barbara broke the quiet. "It's a good thing we'd planned to stay here a couple of nights. Maybe he'll come back."

"The way he'd march off in the middle of hostile desert country," I said glumly, "I'm not so sure."

"We might as well go ahead and do the errands we'd planned," Barbara said. "There's nothing more we can do here."

"Maybe we ought to leave his things here," I suggested. "So he'll know the site if he comes back. There's nothing else we have that says 'home'." Home in the form of the Chinook would naturally roll away and be gone that day. Of course that's what Felix was probably trying to get away from.

"Good idea."

So we drove away, leaving the picnic table adorned with Felix's little bowl filled with food and his orange blanket draped over the seat. At least he could smell "Felix."

If he did come back.

On our way out of the campground, Barbara reported Felix's disappearance at the entrance office. They noted it without comment.

We drove to nearby shopping centers to get groceries and other witless chores. We did it all with a minimum of words.

What was there to say?

After a time I said, "Why don't we go back to the campground for lunch. Maybe he's shown up."

"I kind of doubt it," Barbara replied. "It would be more likely tonight." Perhaps she wanted to put off what might be the inevitable.

"We can't lose anything," I offered.

"All right."

We didn't gain anything either. Not a sign of Felix. The food was gone from his bowl but I imagined the seagulls had quickly dispatched that.

After lunch we set out in search of some supplies on our long-term list. By now we seemed to be going to shopping centers because we couldn't think of anything else to do. Maybe I began to feel they were an appropriate purgatory to punish me for my carelessness. "I knew better," I said. "He didn't know better."

"He thought he did," Barbara said quietly.

"But that's why we have to act as guardians for the creatures," I commented. "We know what the poor things don't know."

That sent us both back into silence.

Down the road we passed a gas dealer's where yesterday we had refilled our propane tank. I felt a welling-up inside me. The swift kick of memory: This was where the woman clerk had commented on what a beautiful cat Felix was. This whole thing of losing him was all beginning to feel a bit like the death of a love affair. As with those experiences, reminders were all about—to remind one of pleasures and bonds that no longer existed. Maybe it wasn't as bad as losing a person. But it sure as hell was sad enough. I felt the tears start to fill my eyes. I fought them. No, I said to myself, I won't cry yet. In time. In time.

"Are you all right?" Barbara asked. I could tell she wasn't feeling any better.

"Yes," I said. "It's just that we've come all this way. We watched him all the time. We're right at the Pacific. Then we lose him."

"After all," Barbara said, "he's not a person." But that was no consolation for either of us. We already knew how much we'd miss his soft, undemanding presence.

We both sat still for a good while as I drove on. Finally Barbara commented, "At least he can survive. It's a pleasant place to be."

"Yes," I agreed, scanning the seaside, urban countryside. "He probably couldn't have picked a better place to live."

Then it dawned on me that we were beginning to face the inevitable—to talk about Felix like he wasn't coming back. We might never again see the dignified, furry little creature who had shared this trek.

The afternoon oozed on like those times in life you wish would just be over. Yet you know you can't hide or put the ache aside. It has to be lived with—like a torn muscle. Eventually there will be healing. In the meantime though—it hurts. All the time.

At dusk we drove back toward the campground. Our hopes began to rise. Surely Felix would show up for supper. He wouldn't miss that.

As the vehicle threaded its way down the road toward our campsite I saw something dart across the blacktop. "What was that?" I called.

"A cat," Barbara cried.

We stopped. I turned so the headlights shone into the bushes.

"Oh," we both said softly. It was a cat certainly. With yellow tiger markings.

We drove on. Another cat sat by the side of the road. But this one was gray. "Hey," I said but didn't go on; this cat was gray all over. No white markings at all.

Our headlights swept into our campsite. Nothing. No Felix. Just his empty food bowl and untouched blanket—in vigil for his absent presence.

"I thought he'd be here," I said slowly.

"I did too," Barbara agreed. "I thought surely he'd come back to eat."

We sat without words for quite a good while.

When faced with glum dead time it's always better to do *something*. "I've got to make a phone call to Aunt Ruth," I said. My cat-mentor aunt lived in Los Angeles. "Let's go up by the office so I can do that and you can ask the ranger if anyone has seen Felix."

"Yes," murmured Barbara.

It was not going to be any easy task to tell cat-loving Aunt Ruth that Felix was gone. But there was no point in delaying it. All the way out to California my telephone progress reports to Ruth had always opened with her asking, "How's the cat?" Before she even asked about *us*.

Aunt Ruth offered what solace she could. Cats do roam—as Adlai Stevenson had pointed out.

Barbara's news was less consoling. The ranger reported that a number of cats, escaped from their traveling homes, had taken up residence in the park. "That explains the cats we saw when we drove in. The ranger said there were five of them."

"Six, now," I muttered through clenched teeth.

We drove back to the campsite.

This time the headlights picked up a couple of glimpses of cat fur and cat eyes. We ignored them. We pulled in to our spot. As I started to turn off the headlights Barbara shouted, "Look!"

Over by the bushes sat a gray cat.

Did this one have white markings?

It did!

I jumped out, ran over and grabbed Felix. I don't think he was going any-where. But I wasn't taking any chances. I held him tight and stroked his long fur.

Barbara patted his head. Finally she said, "He may be hungry."

"Yes," I agreed.

Barbara rubbed the top of his skull fondly. Felix looked up with the content, appreciative expression he always showed for such stroking.

"We're glad you're back, Felix," Barbara said—not just to the cat—but to the world in general.

What more was there to say?

While most books place the dedication at the beginning,
I chose the end—as filmmakers do.
Because then the reader can know what has transpired.
So this is for Barbara who made the trip the great pleasure it was.

0-595-29217-8

Dear Don

Each man and woman who occupies the office of Church Warden brings a uniqueness to the position and task, from which we all benefit. You have brought a warmth and sensitivity which has melted so much of the traditional "coldness" of Cathedrals. I will always be grateful to you for that.

Joe

Christ Church Cathedral
Hamilton, Ontario   Advent 1981

Portrait of a Woman

Portrait of a Woman

Herbert O'Driscoll

Anglican Book Centre
Toronto, Canada

1981
The Anglican Book Centre
600 Jarvis Street
Toronto, Ontario
Canada M4Y 2J6

Printed in Canada

Library of Congress Cataloging in Publication Data

O'Driscoll, Herbert.
Portrait of a woman.
1. Mary, Blessed Virgin, Saint — Meditations.
I. Title.
BT608.5.037   232.91   81-9026
ISBN 0-919030-70-X   AACR2

for Don, Evelyn, Jim,
Lesley, Mary Jane, Patrick,
and Virginia
whose gifts created
the time to tell this story

Contents

Contents

There was a maid in Nazareth;
  Rich with a child was she;
This be my prayer,that day by day
  Christ be in me.

There was a man all crucified;
  Him every eye did see;
My heart that cruel hill, his cross
  My living tree.

There as a king whom death did make
  Prisoner, yet came he free;
He will, if I but own him Lord,
  Arise in me.

Blows there a mighty wind, a fire
  Binding yet setting free,
Making me one with other hearts
  All loving thee.

Mine then for faith this child and man,
  Life won from death in strife;
This be my way and this my truth;
  This be my life.

Herbert O'Driscoll
Munich, June 1980

Preface

This book is an attempt to tell the story of Mary, our Lord's mother. Anyone who sets out to do this must use the word "attempt" because there are limitations none can escape. These severe limitations lie in the extreme paucity of information in the gospels about our Lord's mother.

There follows a list of the scriptural references which we have in the gospels.

Luke, chapters 1 and 2

The annunciation to Mary
Her visit to Elizabeth
The birth of her child
The circumcising of her child
The presentation of her child in the temple
The visit to Jerusalem twelve years later

Matthew, chapter 2

The visit of the Magi
The slaughter of the innocents
The flight into Egypt

John 2:1-11

The wedding at Cana

Mark 6:1-6

A reference to Mary on the occasion of Jesus' visit to Nazareth

Mark 3:31-35

Luke 8:19-21

Matthew 12:46-50

Her visit to Jesus at Capernaum

John 19:25-27

Mary at the Cross

13

Acts 1:12-14

Mary is with the others in the upper room in Jerusalem after the Ascension

Revelation 12:1-6

St John's dream of "a woman clothed with the sun."

Luke 11:27-28

An indirect reference to her in a remark made to Jesus.

In spite of this very small amount of evidence, the person of our Lord's mother has assumed a very great place in the life of the Christian community. Admittedly this is true in some parts of that community more than in others, but in every Christian tradition there is an appreciation of Mary, an instinctive wish to know her and to learn from her life. It is as if the severe limitations of evidence about her have the very opposite effect than the expected, that by the slenderness of material we are haunted and intrigued, and want to know more about her.

The wish to know more has left ample traces of itself in history. Marian writing, story telling, liturgical material, now form a vast body of writing. It varies greatly in quality. Some of it is scriptural and majestic, such as the prayer "Ave Maria" (Hail Mary), or the great song we call "Magnificat." Some of it is created by the determination of early Christian generations to discern hints of her existence and her role in the Old Testament. Some is legend, as we find it in a second century writing called the Book of James or the *Protoevangelium*.

Beyond such things is the rich world of popular devotion which has gathered around the figure of Mary. Perhaps best known of all is the method of meditation which is called the Rosary. Throughout the last decade or so, when many were swept up in the exotic attractions of eastern religion, it was sad to realize that many western Christians had completely forgotten, or perhaps had never known, the availability of a resource such as the Rosary to fulfill their very human need for a technique of meditation or to be, for those who sought it, a Christian mantra.

In addition to these levels of Marian religion, and for many the crown of all else, are the great teachings or dogmas which the Christian church has at various times brought forward on her behalf. The three of these which should be mentioned are the doctrine of her Virginity, the doctrine of her Immaculate Conception, and the doctrine of her Assumption.

It is not my wish here to go into a doctrinal discussion of these things, for the very good reason that I am not fitted to do so. But I wish to emphasize that all the above teachings about our Lord's mother were present in the life of the Christian church for centuries before any were lifted to the level of dogma by any part of the church. The teaching about Mary's virginity has of course been with us from the beginning as part of Luke's gospel. However, criticism of such teachings, on such grounds as "there is no evidence of this in the Bible" or "why did it take until the nineteenth or twentieth century to discover this?" entirely miss the point that the teachings, whatever else, reflect a deep and ancient stream of what I will call Christian instinct rather than Christian thinking.

Speaking of Christian instinct—one of the good things to emerge from the welter and turmoil of the last two decades is a realization that reality is richer than mere rationality. Many strands of human experience, perhaps most obviously the work of Carl Jung, have contributed to our belated recognition that knowing and learning and growing are composed of far more than the cerebral. We have come to realize that we draw too on the elements in us which well up from what we call the unconscious—dreams, intuition, imagination, emotions, instincts. It would be foolish to claim that this is original to our time; rather it is something eternally true but often lost and found again in the great rhythms of history and human affairs, that is now being rediscovered.

The fascination that many Christians feel for Mary is then of both worlds: of observable scripture and elusive legend. When we have made our choices about what we regard as worthwhile or worthless in the vast world of Marian devotion and

15

theology, we are still faced with the fact that it exists, pro-lifically, endlessly creative, and that it brings into Christian experience much beauty—providing a door which attractively and gently can lead us to contemplate the mystery of love and suffering, and finally bring us to the love of Christ himself.

Sometimes criticism of certain levels of devotion to Mary points out the ease with which it can become a focus for the return of pre-Christian concepts of the goddess, the Earth Mother. I doubt that we can or indeed need to deny such con-nections. When St John tells us of his vision of a woman cloth-ed with the sun (Revelation, chapter 12) he is describing something which any Graeco-Roman reader could easily envi-sion as he read or listened. In the cities of the Nile and of Mesopotamia, in the cities of the western Empire of that time, in Jerusalem itself, her images stood bearing a score of names and variously communicating everything from maternity and creativity to sexuality and the erotic.

But even when we have sounded this warning, we once again have to ask why these elements of feminine divinity in human experience are so resilient that they can even use the pathetically imprecise outline which we possess of Mary to release once again all the fears of the feminine mode of divinity that are waiting to be wakened in Christian belief.

One cannot write the last line or two without alluding to one of the great facts of our lifetime. I hesitate to use jargon phrases such as women's liberation or the women's movement because they are incomplete and tend to parody something deeper and finer. Rather let me say that in our lifetime the great covenant made between the two kinds of human being on this planet, one male and the other female, is in process of being refashioned. As the process goes on, Christians, whatever their attitude toward this change, are all seeking for images around which they can focus the new thoughts and arguments and insights that this new dialogue is creating.

I am convinced that there is a "fulness of time" factor in history. What could be more natural if history is God's domain! I cannot but feel that we must now seriously consider what significance the person of our Lord's mother has for us all. I think it would be tragic if, because some traditions have long emphasized her role in salvation, others refuse to assign her any significant role at all. I am convinced that an even deeper element within us than theology is bringing her face into focus again. Words are difficult to capture this intuition.

At many levels today, one of which is sexuality, human nature is in seach of itself. If we are Christian, we are committed to the belief that this search does not go on in an empty universe. We know that Christ is the pattern of our humanity. We are fond of saying that he did not merely become *a* man but that he became *man*—living fully our human nature. We know that in his human nature he mirrors, as do all of us, elements of humanity both masculine and feminine. Yet in recent years there seems to be a search for some door through which woman's yearning for the divine can be mediated by a figure undeniably and fully female, a figure who can be the vehicle for femaleness in its search for deity, to the same degree that Jesus can be appropriated by any man as reflecting fully his maleness. This may well be a great heresy. If so, so be it. There may well be a way through it that I cannot see. Undeniably the question is present.

This little book does not try to create a thesis as to how the Blessed Virgin Mary can be that figure. Even if I wished to do so, I could not write such a book without a great deal more reading and study. I cannot claim that I seek anything as definite as a thesis. At a much less exalted level I am following a hunch. It could be put in one simple and very unscholarly sentence. I believe that this strange and ambiguous age in which I find myself is somehow Mary's time.

If there is any truth in this hunch, I want to serve her cause by attempting to tell her story, even if my telling it achieves nothing more than bringing about a better and fuller telling.

I began by looking carefully at the references listed at the beginning of this preface. I then read the main traditions of the first two centuries which have been handed down about Mary's life. They are chiefly about her birth and her death. I have tried to differentiate between what could have happened and what manifestly is pious story telling. For instance, it is perfectly possible, in the absence of evidence to the contrary, that Mary was born in Jerusalem. On the other hand I doubt very much that Mary as a child spun scarlet thread in the temple while the architects of Herod completely rebuilt it around her, as the apocryphal Book of James suggests. I prefer, for instance, to believe St Augustine when he says in the fifth century that nobody knows what Mary looked like, than to believe Epiphanis in the eighth century when he describes her features in almost photographic detail. As one to whom the great shrine at Knock in the west of Ireland was familiar, I believe that there are those who have been vouchsafed visions of Mary, and that those visions have resulted in healing and holiness for unnumbered people.

Again, when the vast repository of beauty and terror which we call Christian tradition, the corporate memory of all Christians before me, tells me of Mary's virginity, of her immaculate conception, and of her assumption into heaven, I believe that truths have been preserved for me which, though I cannot fully explain nor define them, I neglect to my loss. The question about whether these mysteries should or should not have been formed into dogmas is quite another and is one that need not concern us here.

The main part of this book is my attempt to tell the story of the relationship which existed between Mary and her son Jesus. In so far as anyone can presume to do this at all, I have tried to express the human feelings which she as a perfectly normal human being *could have* experienced. The key word in my mind is *could*. These pages are how it could have been. The theme we are dealing with is sacred for Christians. We are not blithely and vulgarly attempting to reveal secrets of that long ago relationship hitherto unrevealed to the Christian church! As with any great theme the writer of the story or the producer of the play has to come to the task with certain assumptions, which at the same moment make possible his telling of the story but also limit that telling and make other and subsequent tellings necessary.

I have assumed on the basis of my own very fallible reading of the gospel that, at the very least, Mary found her son's decisions and actions extremely difficult to understand and to accept.

I have assumed for purposes of this telling that she was as tantalized and mystified by the images Jesus used when speaking of the kingdom as were any of his disciples. To maintain, merely because they lived with him, that the first disciples and such individuals as Mary were able to comprehend a vision that twenty centuries of Christian experience and thought and worship have not exhausted, seems to me the height of unreality.

There is one further assumption I wish to make with particular reverence and care. I cannot help but see that in the relationship between Mary and Jesus, at least in the years of his ministry, there were some periods of breakdown that neither could repair. And so their relationship contained the mingled intimacy and fulfillment coupled with guilt and estrangement that characterize all human relationships.

Again it is my assumption that Mary discovered her son and his love in the same way that each of us in our time does—in the community of those who believe in his risen life, break bread and drink wine in his name, sing his praise, and touch one another's lives with his love.

A word now about some key choices which anyone writing about Mary must make.

I have chosen to read as literal truth that Mary's womb was quickened to life by divine action other than the divine action of normal human sexual intercourse. I do not understand it, but I believe that its inclusion in scripture is for a divine purpose.

I have assumed, because Joseph does not appear in the years of Jesus' ministry, that he died at some time before those years began.The fact that we know of the large building development at nearby Sepphoris about this time, gives me what of course can be nothing more than a possible set of circumstances for Joseph's death.

I have assumed that Jesus was not only Mary's firstborn but her only child, and that the four brothers and the sisters mentioned in the gospels are in fact cousins. I have linked two other possibilities for the purpose of my story, neither without some evidence. The first is that Mary the wife of Clopas may have been the Virgin Mary's sister-in-law. The second possibility is that the children of Mary and Clopas (two of whom are named in the gospel and bear the same names as those referred to elsewhere as Jesus' "brothers") may well be those among whom the solitary cousin Jesus grew and played, and that they may have regarded him as their "brother." Language usage of the time makes such blurring of relationships quite possible.

However, these things are irresolvable and have to do with the framework of the story. The heart of the matter is the human relationship that existed between this particular woman and her son. Did it have elements such as we all know only too well in our own relationships? To be human it must have had such elements. To explore these is what I set out to do. The relationship could as well have been explored if one had taken different choices about such things as Mary's virginity, about subsequent children, or about the time of Joseph's death. For this particular telling the question is about the feelings and reactions of a woman as she tries to be true to herself, to her perceptions of reality, and to those she loved.

This book is no more a life of Mary than the book which John Mark wrote was a life of Jesus. It has become commonplace to say that almost one-third of Mark's book is given to the last week in Jesus' ministry, and that this is so because that last week is the heart of the matter. In rather the same way, I think, we may be able to say that the reasons why any treatment of Mary must find itself heavily weighted toward the period of her child's birth and earliest childhood, is simply that her pre-eminence in the eyes of early Christians depended on her role as the bearer of the child Jesus. Beside that, all else was secondary. If this is true, it may seem somewhat callous, and even in today's eyes, chauvinist, but at least it is understandable. The part she had played gave her significance. In fact, the immensity of her role may very quickly have so isolated her from normal relationships that it may never have occurred to anyone that she had experienced a full and rich spectrum of feelings and thoughts during the thirty years or so leading up to the final three eventful years.

This then is an attempt not at biography but at portraiture. As with all portraits, certain choices of approach have been made. Because of this, other equally possible approaches have had to be rejected. But then the essence of our humanity and of hers is that no portrait entirely captures its subject. It reveals only a glimpse of what must always remain a mystery. The important thing is what a portrait is for. If it is a good portrait, it will draw us toward the subject, deepening our awareness and even making possible sometimes a relationship. When the portrait is of that which is most sacred, as in this attempt at portraiture, my hope is to make possible that contemplation of the sacred which we call devotion, a devotion offered to a woman who has for millions of Christians become our Lady, and whose eternal privilege it is to turn our eyes from the contemplation of her own loveliness to the greater glory of her son our Lord.

The Presence

And the angel came in unto her, and said, Hail, thou that art highly favoured, the Lord is with thee: blessed art thou among women. And when she saw him, she was troubled at his saying, and cast in her mind what manner of salutation this should be. Luke 1:28–29

At the heart of all reality, said the Greek story-teller, there is the Word. It is alive eternally. It lies waiting to be spoken, and when it is spoken it will show us all things. It will bring meaning and illumination and light to those who hear it. On the island of Patmos, or it may have been among the hills and valleys that surround the city of Ephesus, another story-teller continued this tale. The Word, says the aged disciple John, has been spoken. There are those who have received it. They have not merely heard it; they have touched it. And they have touched it because of the mode of its coming to humanity. The Word, said John, has become flesh.

Sixty years before John began to tell his story, and approximately five hundred miles south-east of Ephesus, a girl carrying a waterpot in one hand while supporting another on her head, was picking her way down a pathway outside a village on the southern slope of the escarpment that linked the highlands of Galilee and the rich valley of Esdraelon. She walked slowly, enjoying the sweep of the countryside, finding it fascinating after the sandy hills and narrow streets of Jerusalem where she had spent her childhood.

She approached the well, and her eyes turned from the blazing sunlight to the shadowed cool depths of the precious water. Light glittered and shimmered as she gently disturbed the surface. She had done this a thousand times in her domestic responsibilities, but this time there was a difference. It was not something seen; rather it was something felt. It dwelt in the brilliant play of sun and shadow, in the flashing and changing patterns of the well's surface, in the surrounding silence now strangely no longer silent. Aware of a presence, and being fearful, she fled.

We speak so casually of the presence of God. We assume certain things of it, that it is nice, that it is soothing, encouraging, affirmative. This of course is a reflection of our wishes, and indeed there are times when the presence of God is thus. But to describe the presence of God in this way is like describing the ocean as calm, the wind as a whisper, or fire as warming. There can be terror to the presence of God. The fact that we sometimes feel this terror, its demand, its vocation, its cost, is precisely the measure of how clear is our understanding of God.

Her instinct was to share the experience with the man who would soon be her husband. Joseph himself was a gentle man, sensitive to Presence, rich in dreams, open to the voices which occupy human silence. Yet she kept the moment to herself, probably with the instinct that stops us naming a dread lest we give it greater substance.

One day months later, into a silence and a solitude, the Presence came again. She was suddenly aware of it, aware of being encountered from an incalculable distance. Yet it stood so near that she felt occupied by its gentle yet terrible energy. She was conscious again of the deep waters of the well, only this time its depths revealed eyes which held her gaze and probed her own inmost depths, revealing, searching, possessing all. She struggled prisoner like, whimpering in fear yet crying out with ecstasy.

Aeons of time passed, aeons echoing with generations proclaiming her blessedness. Before her moved histories and empires, legions of the past, principalities of immeasurably distant futures. Through all of them it seemed to her she moved as queen. Then it was all gone. In its place there swam into her vision the small square window through which she looked across the Galilean fields. The world remained the same. Seed time and harvest, summer and winter, the fish leaping in the lake beyond the hills, the eternal cycle continued around her.

But Mary knew that the reality around her, solid though it seemed, had been penetrated by a greater. She had felt the divine visitation which in some way comes to us all. What had been asked of her was unique, and yet an echo of it reaches all of us if only we have ears to hear. She had been asked to offer herself to the divine will, to become a servant. She had made her choice, as we all must. Fully and freely she had said Yes. For those who say Yes nothing is ever the same again.

A Shared Responsibility

Then said Mary unto the angel, How shall this be, seeing that I know not a man! And the angel answered and said unto her, The Holy Ghost shall come upon thee, and the power of the Highest shall overshadow thee. Luke 1:34–35

They faced each other on the hillside, the village spread out behind them. She observed his face, seeing the pain in his eyes, watching his lips shape words that changed before being spoken and so remained unsaid. She knew that she had wounded him deeply.

There was so much he could understand, even more than some men. As she had guessed he would, he accepted the reality of the Presence and the vision. Yet everything in his upbringing, in his manhood, his self-image, his understanding of his role in their society—everything rebelled against the expected child. In his eyes was the anticipated pain of community contempt, the snide remarks he would not hear, his fear for her if he abandoned her.

They spoke of their contract to marry. Already it was effective and public knowledge. It allowed them to be together, as they were at this moment. This could be set aside; there were many precedents. Society always has methods of saving face. Unfortunately, while saving face for him was a matter only of a few legal arrangements, for her it was not so simple. Above all there was the child. For a moment his mind tried to come to grips again with the things she had told him. Was it possible that she was in the grip of some madness? She came from the south, from Judea with its seething cosmopolitan world, its many fanaticisms of religion and politics, its dreams of a messiah. Was it possible that her young and intense mind had removed her a step from reality?

As they stand together, bonded by their love for one another, speaking of a life as yet unborn, they become archetypes of unnumbered couples in our own century who speak of an unborn life come suddenly from their mutual passion. They speak of it in cars, in restaurants, in apartments. They realize that they hold over the unborn life the power of life and death. Sometimes death is chosen in an agony of guilt. Terrible as this is, it is not so terrible as when the decision is taken with a detachment and casualness that reduces life to nothing, and bitterly wounds its Creator.

In pain and confusion they parted, the agony unresolved. Only later would she know the turmoil he experienced as he tried to decide between the ghastly alternatives they faced. Later he would tell her of the agony, of the exhaustion that became restless sleep, of the sleep that changed and deepened and moved him into a part of his life that would always be rich—his dreams. He would try to find words for the Presence, for the voice that is always more for us all than a spoken voice. As he tried to express the experience, the two of them would feel drawn together by this shared mystery. They would realize that the Presence which had approached each of them was the same, the voice that had addressed each of them, the same voice.

He would tell her of his awakening after the dream, of the inexplicable calm after the night, the clarity of the way ahead. They could continue their plans. She spoke of wanting to visit a cousin in the south. He didn't really relish this, but he had learned that he faced in her a mysterious energy that had a way of making her decisions self-fulfilling. What plans they had would necessarily be tentative. In those days many dreaded the possibilities ahead for their province. In Galilee life was reasonably peaceful. Here was a society easy, accepting, peaceful, prosperous. But all around them were the nervous elements of the eastern empire. To the south was Judea, politically unstable yet embroiled in power politics reaching all the way to Rome and Alexandria. To the north in Syria lay Rome's military headquarters, the legions ready at any time to sweep down the nearby highway to Jerusalem. Joseph looked at the girl whose body was alive with something he had to force himself to accept, to try to understand. Before him the future loomed dark with almost incomprehensible choices.

A Search for Understanding

And Mary arose in those days, and went into the hill country with haste, into a city of Juda; And entered into the house of Zacharias, and saluted Elizabeth. Luke 1:39–40

They had had their discussions. She had told Joseph of her experience and had seen in his eyes the turmoil of the emotions coursing through him. As any man of his time Joseph was perfectly aware of the concept of such a birth. Galilee was a cosmopolitan area, rich with the temples, myths, and rites of the Graeco-Roman world. Among them such births were legion, narrated in stories and acted out in sacred rites. But all this made it no easier for Joseph to face the fact that such an event had emerged now from story and ritual into his own everyday life.

So he had looked at her—in his eyes pain and love. She had never forgotten that first conversation. Later he had come to her with the news of his own dream experience, assuring her that he could now affirm hers. But she knew that the enormity of what was happening to both of them was not to be dealt with overnight. She knew too well what they faced. The village they both lived in was an earthy and sometimes brutally harsh community. It would not hesitate to voice its own varied and vivid opinions during the months ahead. Luke notes that she left "with haste." Probably she also left with tears and hurt. If so, she would head instinctively for some source of understanding and sympathy, however far away it was.

As she takes her journey, Mary is a very contemporary figure. Community—our need of it, our seeking for it—is a very complex and varied thing. It need not always be found among those nearest us, although we do in a sense share physical community with them in a thousand practical ways. It may be that in our society of mobility and transience, our deepest community exists with others who may be far away. We seldom see them, but from some intimate moment or shared experience or former period of life, they have become and remain for us kindred spirits. They understand us and we them in the realm of our inward journeying, and even though we cannot share with them a constant community, we feel we can always turn to them, always take up where we left off with them.

For Mary such a source lay to the south, fifty miles away in Judea. There lived Elizabeth and Zachariah. In some ways their world was very different from hers. They were both of a very much older generation, their world the conservative world of the priesthood. But there was one overriding thing which Elizabeth shared with Mary. She was expecting a child, a child whose arrival had been totally beyond their wildest expectations, a child about whose coming there was a sense of the particular, the unexpected, the mysterious.

No wonder, when they met, it was for both women an ecstatic moment. In that world of limited travel (at least for ordinary people) and dangerous roads, to meet at all was an occasion. But to meet at this time, when both were aware of mysterious life within them, when their whole being was oriented to a future unguessed at by either of them only a few short months before, these circumstances lifted their meeting to another level. It seemed to both of them, as they greeted each other, that undefinable and invisible universes were melding together, hidden under their joy and laughter and salutations.

Within Mary and Elizabeth two histories breathed, moved, and grew. Elizabeth was carrying the eternal song of Israel, called prophecy. In John her child, her flesh would sing it again, harsh and high and disturbing. He would go from her into wilderness and isolation. He would face powers and principalities, and would challenge them. He would be butchered like an animal, as so many before him had been when they challenged human will and greed in the name of a higher will.

Within Mary lay hidden a song that would rise from the death of such prophecy. It would rise pure and clean and gentle, and yet by many be found even stronger and more challenging than all that had gone before. It would go from her into a like fate. There would be challenge and reaction, a death even more obscene than that of John. And, though Mary could not know it, there would then be a womb other than hers, a womb of rock, that would open for a birth beyond her imagining.

A Song for All Generations

And Mary said, My soul doth magnify the Lord, And my spirit hath rejoiced in God my Saviour. For he hath regarded the low estate of his handmaiden: for, behold, from henceforth all generations shall call me blessed.   Luke 1:46–48

Locked in each others arms, the two women were aware of each other's life and power and sexuality. They both carried within them that most precious of life's elements, a future being. For Elizabeth there was the exhilaration of a recaptured youthfulness, for Mary the endless horizons of the angelic promises.

It was Elizabeth who first found words, and they were words of mature and loving unselfishness. In spite of her own inner excitement, she is more aware of the younger woman and the other child. "Who am I," Elizabeth cries, "that the mother of my Lord should visit me?" As with all ecstasy and inspiration, it is useless here to analyse, to probe for logic and reason. In that single sentence Elizabeth pre-figures the relationship which will always exist between these two children. Time and time again, with a graciousness that is the mark of his greatness, John will say of Jesus, "He must increase; I must decrease." But this lies in the future.

We all know persons who richly possess the gift of unselfishness, whose first instinct is to enquire for us rather than to speak of themselves, to listen avidly to our tellings, to show concern for our affairs, to rejoice with us and weep with us as if the reason for their existence is to serve us. Sometimes we are shamed by their self-giving. Sometimes, if we are fortunate, we can be enriched by the infection of their loveliness and be changed a little to their likeness.

Breaking away from Elizabeth, Mary is no longer able to contain herself. Suddenly, met by the love in Elizabeth's eyes, held in her arms, Mary for the first time feels accepted and understood. Not even Joseph with his love could so understand and accept. His attempts at acceptance cannot help but be tinged by masculinity threatened, by fear of community contempt, by the burden of social role and image. As well there has been for Mary the tension of the village. But here, far away, someone totally understands. Suddenly all the pent-up feelings of months erupt. Her mind searches madly for words, races through her being, through all the songs that she has ever been taught, and finds a vehicle for her joy.

The song she finds is that of another woman who centuries before celebrated what Mary feels. A thousand years before her, somewhere in these same hills, a woman named Hannah had held in her arms the child she had so desperately longed for. And in her emotion she sang, reaching back even further in time for a song of praise and thanksgiving. Centuries later her song would echo on the lips of Mary.

It is a lovely and terrible song, this "Magnificat," as other ages would come to call it. It would be taken from Mary's lips and be augmented into a mighty anthem, echoing in basilica and cathedral. It would, in the centuries-long monastic round of offices, be the song that welcomed the approach of evening. It would become a centre point around which a jewel called English evensong would revolve. Yet it would also be a dark and terrible song of revolution. It would be quoted in societies moving through social turmoil, on continents seething with a desire for change.

Why this strange mingling of the personal and the political, the heart and the world? Did Mary know, not with her mind but at some level beyond her conscious knowing; did she know that what lay within her would speak, not only to the human heart, but to the disturbing of the world?

The Unborn King

The Lord himself shall give you a sign; Behold, a virgin shall conceive and bear a son, and shall call his name Immanuel.
Isaiah 7:14

In the warm waters of her womb he lay at peace, ceaselessly moving yet perfectly at rest. He occupied a universe of which he was the sole inhabitant. In it he reigned as king. He did not yet know her as woman or as mother, only as life source. Already he is acting out the mystery before which we must continually wonder. The divine dwells in the human, not merely at this particular moment but always, not merely in this woman but in every womb. If there are to be acknowledged circumstances when we must trespass into the womb and take from it its life, then let us do it with the proper sense of awe, and let us at least give this mystery the courtesy of our terror.

Later the child would feed and grow on her love. For now, unborn yet forming, he fed and grew on her life. In this too is a mystery, that God who knows no need has stooped to have need of our poor nature to effect this rich nativity. This dust, chosen by God for our formation in the first moments of creation, is what he now chooses to form the flesh in which we will encounter divinity.

Carried in the silent universe of her womb he will soon descend from these hills of Galilee, pass through the upper valley of the Jordan and be carried south to Judea, journeying in response to the command of an emperor in a world beyond his knowing. Men and women will pass him without knowing. He goes hidden through the world. In a sense God goes forever through time and place hidden, seen only with the eyes of faith.

All these things are signs. Surrounding this fragile humanity, lying within him as he lies within her, is the indescribable glory that we have ever since sought to express. We bring to it our pathetic and groping labels. We speak of "divinity." We intone "light of light" and "very God of very God." We fashion a thousand theologies. We philosophize and debate and excommunicate.

30

In her womb he lay in endless rest yet in endless agitation. If he had chosen our frantic and clever century for incarnation, our eyes would have seen on the medical device we call Sonar Scan his tiny leg upraised, an arm swinging, a head drooping and rising. In spite of all our inventions, we would of course have been blind to the glory beyond all our scanners. Yet even in the baby's rest and motion, we would be seeing the nature of the divine itself, endlessly at peace yet endlessly energetic, ceaselessly creating.

The sole inhabitant of her womb, he dwells in a universe alone. Here too is a sign of the truth we are forever trying to unravel. In a sense he dwells alone, unique in the universe as we know it. He is flesh of our flesh; yet because of his unique relationship with the Father, he is more. He is God of Gods; yet because of his taking our flesh, he is less. Within her womb he reigns in a kind of kingship—supreme, alone, unchallenged. The resources of this inner world, flowing along her umbilicial cord, are for his use alone. Without the nourishment of these resources he will die.

In this lies a sign for our age. No longer child in the womb of his mother, he now lives as lord of that greater womb we call time and history. In it he is, for those who own him, king. In this history, which we inhabit and in which we claim to worship him, he again claims resources for his use. This time it is the resources of the planet. He claims them as surely as he claimed those of his mother's body. He claims them for justice and for redistribution—two purposes which are really one. He demands that we acknowledge the earth's resources to be for his purposes rather than for our own selfish ends. What at our worst we have seen to exist for our thoughtlessness and limitless exploitation, we now are being made to realize exists for his will for the planet and for humanity. He demands that they be used to energize love rather than greed, creativity as well as consumption.

Already, even though unborn, he is a sign of authority. Already his mother is also a sign. Her body is a parable of the world's need and fruitfulness.

An Emperor's Decree

And it came to pass in those days, that there went out a decree from Caesar Augustus, that all the world should be taxed.

Luke 2:1

The machinery of Empire is expensive. Rome is no exception. To keep the creaking cogs of government moving, to clear the Mediterranean of the chronic threat of piracy, to boost the morale of the all-important legions soon to stretch from the west bank of the Euphrates to the Grampian Hills in Britain—all of this demands money. Money is procured from taxes, taxes involve a census taking.

Once taken, the decision has to be communicated across the empire. From Rome the promulgating document for the eastern provinces goes to the coast, then across the Mediterranean to another coast at the mouth of the Orontes, and from there up the valley to headquarters at Antioch. Out of the legate's office it begins its journey by mounted courier to Damascus, then continues south-west along the road which eventually runs north of the Lake of Galilee. At some stage news of the census is carried in the diplomatic pouch along a road which passes within five miles of a village called Nazareth.

Surrounding our private existence is the public and political. Nowadays we treasure the former, leaving the public and political for those who choose what seem to be its brutalities and complexities. Contemporary life, deeply and intensely committed to the personal, to the family and other close relationships, is alienated from the public and institutional levels of life, to our great and growing cost. The intimacy of our Nazareths is treasured. The legions of empire, glimpsed in newspapers, magazines, and television, are dealt with in various ways. They can be switched off, unless of course some sudden violation of peace and order takes place in our city. Even then it can be dismissed as peculiar, an aberration which can and should be dealt with. We presume that suitable laws will be passed, or that the police will act, or that the army or the government will take steps. Something will happen so that we will not have to decide to act or change personally. Yet sometimes a message comes that cannot but affect our lives. It forces us into actions that change us and change the course of our living. Such was the message that came to long ago Nazareth.

Probably they hear the rumour before the proclamation is put up outside the military station in the village. It comes as a shock. She is now near the end of her pregnancy, counting the last weeks, gathering a little store of necessary things, arranging for the help of friends, for assistance during the actual delivery. Now it is all changed. The fact that Joseph has family roots in Judea makes it absolutely necessary that they go south before the census deadline.

Between them and Bethlehem lie eighty-five long and dangerous miles. There will be many travellers. This will make the journey somewhat safer from the ever-present hill bandits. The military patrols crucified them whenever they captured them, but there were always many more to take their places in the hills. Once again Joseph faces an agonizing decision. The ride will be desperately dangerous for her and for the child at this late stage of pregnancy. All they can do is trust that this new turn of events is for a purpose. Joseph may well recall the ceaseless journeys of generations before him — children brought to birth on the edge of Sinai and the wilderness, or in another age in the desert sands, as prisoners march east to Babylon.

Unknown to both Mary and Joseph, other travellers have already set out on an even longer journey, one that has begun on the high plateaux of Persia and will end with kings kneeling at her feet in a far away cave. Unknown to her and to Joseph the night sky above them is moving to the rare conjunction of Jupiter and Saturn. It will speak to philosophers of a ruler born for an age in crisis. They know none of this. Neither do we know how other journeys will converge on our lives and we on theirs, as we travel into our unknown future.

The Road to the South

For ye know the grace of our Lord Jesus Christ, that, though he was rich, yet for your sakes he became poor, that ye through his poverty might become rich.   2 Corinthians 8:9

The river road is the most travelled way. To pass through Samaria is to risk at least unpleasantness. Day by day they make measured progress because of her inability to take too much movement. The palm trees and houses of Jericho appear in the distance like a promised land. From the lovely green and shaded city in its oasis setting, they move out again across the widening valley floor. To their right they can see the long high escarpment which runs north and south down the backbone of Israel. They must climb that, and in the dead heat.

A great part of the human experience is obligation. There are many levels to its demands. There is of course obligation to others, most immediately to those who are part of us—parents, children, the extended circle of our own flesh and blood. This obligation we assume naturally, sometimes resenting it when we are weary, but then knowing guilt because of this very resentment. From there flow the widening circles of obligation—friends, customers, clients, teachers, employers, authority figures of many kinds. At some stage relationship disappears into organization, obligation into obedience. Now we experience the impact on us, not of human beings but of structures. These are mediated to us by people, but gradually we become more aware of a huge background of communication networks, distant faceless decision makers, computers, social and political factors that seem totally beyond our control and often totally insensitive to our wishes or our well-being.

Such is the distant decision which sends the unborn child on his way from Nazareth to Bethlehem. It also decrees that in the final weeks of her pregnancy, both he and his mother are endangered. As well, it burdens Joseph with the sense of helplessness and seething resentment that many of us know only too well as we struggle to survive among the great structures affecting our lives in our time.

They continue to head east. Turning away from the shimmering blue of the nearby Dead Sea, they rest before beginning the first part of their climb. Almost three thousand feet above them, hidden by the curve of the mountain, lies Jerusalem. During the long hours as they climb, she and Joseph may sing together the songs they would have learned as children, songs composed for the very journey they are now taking up toward the city.

I will lift up mine eyes unto the hills:
O whence cometh my help?
The Lord shall preserve thy going out and thy coming in, from this time forth for evermore.

As she sings, she becomes aware that, like many of her people's songs, the words are true for all people and all times. For some reason it seems insufficient merely to sing of personal joy, though there is more of this than she can measure. Somehow this birthing, which is even now changing her daily, is also a birthing that will change the world. The thought, too immense to be a statement, remains for her a question.

None of us find it easy to consider ourselves or our affairs to be particularly significant beyond ourselves, least of all to be world-changing. In most of our lives our ambition and self-image is placed modestly and personally. We seek to secure a little of the elusive mystery called happiness. We hope to avoid the more terrible crosses of our imagination. We have whole languages and industries to help us. We speak of "personal growth," form "marriage encounter" programs, read paper backs on survival, on maturity, on wholeness, sexuality, death. And indeed none of these things are insignificant for our humanity. Yet we avoid to our peril the other thrust, the external adventure, the creation around us, the political, the city, the institutional, the world. Mary is a peasant girl, yet she is at this time given a greatness and a grace to include in her reflections not only the personal circle of her own existence, but the far greater circles of human power and structure which her unborn son will claim for his own in centuries to come.

An Unknown Gentleness

Fear not: for I have redeemed thee, I have called thee by thy name; thou art mine. When thou passest through the waters, I will be with thee.   Isaiah 43:1–2

Her womb is the first ocean of his journeying. There will be other waters. Years in the future they will sweep over him as he lies curled and sleeping in the prow of a fishing boat on a stormy lake. Now, curled in her womb, peace is uninterrupted. There are no shrill voices demanding that he act, no pleadings for his intervention.

When did the waters leave her body, calling him to the next stage of his journey within her? Were they brought by the constant jarring movement of the beast clambering up the winding road, carrying her to Bethlehem? If so, she would have turned to other, older women on the same road. What gentle hand, experienced eye, served her need by the roadside? What voice counted the hours and quietly told Joseph he had just so much time to find shelter for the coming birth? Whose hand felt her body and saw the outline of the Son of God as he turned for his coming into the world?

We are all midwives to the divine birth, most frequently in ignorance. We who travel with others the roads of our pilgrimages constantly find ourselves called on for help. The voice, tremulous on the telephone, revealing fear or depression or loneliness, to which we give our sometimes grudging half-hour. The business colleague, half broken by the tensions of the day, with whom we have to curb the temptation to be short and almost contemptuous, our shortness being in turn the measure of our own tension. These are the companions on the road who suddenly lurch to the side, their vulnerability revealed. Sometimes, from our gesture of concern given often from our own weariness and our own weakness, there is born in them the things which are divine, the things of hope, courage, of love itself. Without realizing it, we tend them and so become the unwitting midwives of God's life and love.

When the waters of her womb had gone, the child had no choice but to prepare for birth. To remain in this tiny world of flesh, even if that were possible, would now be fatal. So it is with all of us on our journey. In jobs, careers, relationships, there comes a time when the waters of fullness pass. We feel a dryness, an emptiness, a realization that we must act or we will taste something of death. We must decide to set about being born toward the next stage of our existence.

There are times when we, like Mary, must become the recipients of help on our journey. But we, like her, do not wish to be the focus of need, to call attention to our moment of weakness or sickness or exhaustion. And yet so often from such a time, and from such a touch of love and care from others, often quite unexpected, we find ourselves helped toward giving birth to things that we did not know lay within us, and the experience enables us to continue on the road to whatever Bethlehem we are bound for.

For a brief while Mary rests by the roadside. A thousand feet above her, on the crown of the great outcropping where Jerusalem stands, a priest reads from a scroll in the temple. In these scrolls the waters figure again and again as the source of life. From the waters came the newborn earth, called into being by the Creator. From the waters come Noah and his ark, Moses in his cradle. From the waters come a people for God's possession and promise. All this the priest will read in the temple, while eastward in the blazing afternoon a Galilean girl resumes her frantic search for shelter, so that she may give birth to the child for whose coming the waters of her body have been parted by God.

The Fulness of Time

Unto us a child is born, unto us a son is given.   Isaiah 9:6

In one sense the terrible journey which must now be taken through her body is the last step of an infinite journey. To grope for language to express immeasurable distances is pointless. The journey of this now waiting birth passage is beyond categories of space. The distance is measurable only in terms of that infinite gulf between humanity and divinity, between time and eternity.

We will never cease to look for language to express this mystery. To it cultures will bring the complexity of their philosophies. We will, if we are wise, take refuge in language which is the music of thought rather than its mechanics. We will sing "the Word became flesh...and we beheld his glory." Or wiser still, we will be silent, allowing angels to sing as one did to Mary months before this moment, "fear not...for the power of the Almighty will overshadow thee...and thou shalt bring forth a son."

The moment we hear such music we are made aware of the unimaginable qualitative gulf to be crossed as the divine moves toward our humanity by the only means possible, the body of this woman. And yet in the moment of realizing the gulf we see it closed, bridged, reduced to nothing by this child. Humanity and God wait together, poised between womb and world, preparing for the agony and joy of birth.

She moves through Bethlehem with Joseph, their quickening pace belying the calm they are both assuming in the face of continued failure to find shelter. The rhythms of her body tell her that the vision in far away Galilee is nearing fulfilment in this frantic and terrible strangeness. But eventually there is the warmth of shelter, the blessed relief of rest, a little food and drink, then the sinking into waves of pain sweeping through her body.

The child too moves forward toward the unkown, taking the journey we have all experienced in fear and pain. We know from psychology that the terrors of this passage will remain with him always at some level of consciousness. They will become, as they do with all of us, the unconscious reference for all pain and fear, remembered only in deepest dreams. This pain will be felt again in a garden where he will pray, convulsed with fear. It will sweep over him on a hilltop he has never seen. This sense of being bound will be felt again among enemies to come. As he now moves in her body, he lies for a moment entombed, until she with her loving will opens the tomb of flesh, enabling her son to be born, ushering into the world the glorious possibility of our resurrection.

The straw is red with her blood. It gleams on her body, on Joseph's hands, on the wet and glistening skin of the child. It is the price of her self-giving, the price of Joseph's faithfulness, the price of life. We tend to associate blood with our endings rather than our beginnings. Blood is associated with pain, injury, death. Much Christian imagery speaks easily of blood in relation to the cost of our salvation. It links blood with the man, the crucified prisoner, the pierced side, the stigmata. Yet blood is also the mark of our childhood and his, our very birth and his. Neither our life nor his are free even at first breath. Both are made possible by a cost paid by the love of another. We do not take our first breath before we are debtors to love. For endless ages stretching from this moment, his blood will become the price of our salvation.

The Humility of God

In this was manifested the love of God toward us, because that God sent his only begotten Son into the world, that we might live through him. 1 John 4:9

Like all of us, he became aware of her breast as the source of life. In its fullness it moved above him, filling his emerging vision, a sun by day, a moon by night, bringing warmth and nourishment and peace. He received it first in the dim-lit cave under the ridge with the restless town above them. To this day Bedouin women nurse children in these same caves, finding shelter as they move hither and yon across the countryside.

This new-born child would become aware of her first as the only "thou" in his universe. Very soon he would recognize another pair of hands, a body harder and stronger than hers, a deeper sound, no less loving but different. But now, swaddled against the night chill, there was only she.

He would share our humanity in the intensity of his seeking her milk. Born to our state, he is inhabited by an immediate fear of dying, a literal thirst for life. The first terrible lessons are being learned about this fragile human state. Because God has emptied himself, the babe he has become must now look to this woman to be filled. Because God has set aside his power, this woman of earth must now empower the child God has become.

By this tableau which we see in the shadows, this woman holding this child, we are being introduced to an insight totally at odds with what we think of as reality. We are looking at ultimate power revealing itself as ultimate trust and dependence. Our human view of power involves the direction of others, personal independence, invulnerability. If what we believe about this child is true, then we are being taught by God that there is a mysterious power beyond our human concept of it, a mystery calling us to risk living a mystery if we wish to discover it. The applications are endless. In the daily stress of modern life, it is the person who is ready to acknowledge particular times of powerlessness who is truly powerful. The person able to lose dignity is the man or woman most likely to keep it; the person ready to acknowledge the need for help is most likely to achieve a goal. Years later the grown man will say to us, "Whosoever shall lose his life, shall preserve it."

In here the light is dim and flickering, yet outside the skies are lit by legions of light reflected in the frightened eyes of distant shepherds. Soon, impelled by an inarticulate adoration, they will seek this cave, probing its shadows for her and for the child.

As she crouches in these shadows, a woman suckling her child, she is a familiar figure of their harsh world. Yet their instincts tell them she is more. There is here a mystery. In lighting the way for these men, the skies have not explained it but only revealed its presence. Men will kneel in the shadows of ten thousand caves, grander, cleaner, higher. There will be caves with other names—grottoes, shrines, chapels, churches, basilicas, cathedrals. One and all they will be surrogates of this fetid place. They will stand more glorious, be graced with precious gifts, symbolize cultures, powers, dynasties, empires. Yet not one of them will possess the glory flickering along these cobwebbed walls. Not all their choirs, psalm chanting, and anthem singing will capture the sounds of this night—the voice of Mary murmuring magnificats we have never known, the fretful protest of the child being taken from one breast to the other.

She and the child are familiar. Before the familiar we stand expressing our joy and appreciation. But there is here something more than the familiar. There is here a majesty, a mystery that draws our knees to the dust, that inculcates a holy and joyous fear.

Holding her child this peasant girl of Galilee will change and grow. She will hold him in countless attitudes, gaze upon the world in countless faces, be clothed with countless forms of dress. She will become a lady of Byzantium or of Renaissance Italy, a Chinese princess, a woman of the African veldt. Yet however she is changed, she will forever continue to do what she is doing in this cave. Forever her arms will encompass the child, forever give him birth, forever nourish him. She is more than Demeter the great earth mother. Mary is *theotokos*, mother of God, and Jesus her child is first among the sons of the morning.

An Acquaintance with Pain

When the fulness of time was come, God sent forth his Son, made of a woman, made under the law.   Galatians 4:4

The cave under the ridge cannot contain him forever. What he has been born to become must now begin the journey. Hidden by God in this humble place, the divine leaven must now begin to move through time and human experience.

It is her task to bring him to his first experience of pain. With Joseph she takes him to the synagogue. It is eight days since his birth, and her body is still healing after fulfilling its unique vocation. Normally this would be an occasion for some gathering of the family. Here there is nobody to share it, at least not on her side. There may have been kinsmen of Joseph. She takes him for circumcision, still unweaned. As she carries him toward the synagogue, her body communicates a distant tremor of something he feels but as yet has little reference to identify. Later he will know it as the fear of suffering, the primeval enemy he will often know.

Her fear in this particular moment distances him from her. He is flesh of her flesh, and yet in this symbolic act of circumcision lies part of the mystery of the eternal difference between them, the difference of masculinity and feminity on which he and she, mother and son, will play a lifelong symphony of complex relationship. If there may lie hidden in his future other women, other relationships, then she as his mother has the power to mould his capacity for such encounters. From her and his dealings with her will come the capacity in later years to be easy and sensitive with women, to sustain serious dialogue with someone at a well at Sychar, to inspire adoration, if not passion, without patronizing or manipulating.

The small synagogue echoes to his high, shrill, whimpering cry, his first moment of searing pain, this time swift and passing. It will be followed by days and nights of discomfort and the quick healing of a child. In years to come she will remember this sharp cry. A greater cry will assail her ears under a darkening sky from crosses gashed across a nightmare landscape. The knife, small, ceremonial, is for a moment stained with his blood. Without knowing it he has given the first tiny element of his body. One day he will offer it totally as sacrifice, giving it to other knives by then full grown to spears.

They and the rabbi exchange the warm rejoicing conversation of such family moments. There is a felt satisfaction about being faithful to ancient tradition, a comfort from conforming. The law has been observed. In this circumcision the child has felt the first steely touch of the law. It is not evil, but it is capable of trapping men and women on a treadmill of religious stagnation. It can enable the Spirit, but it can imprison the Spirit. All this will be felt by the child, will be challenged and wrestled with by the man. By an eternal irony the law will be both his inspiration and his nemesis.

We see it as a moment in their lives because that is how we see all life — in moments. Yet no moment is detached and in itself complete. All moments are connected—a sequence, a pattern, a progression. All moments of passing pain are outriders of a great enemy. All moments of joy and of ecstasy are harbingers and hints of the mystery we call heaven. All moments are the materials of our maturing, the stuff of personhood, the touch of time's fingers as it paints our portrait.

Here at the door of the synagogue, emerging from its shadows to the sunlight, hastily shading the child's eyes, she is burdened by none of this. This is a day of joy and fulfillment. She has a right to this moment, to savour it. She is at this moment the Mother of all our Joys.

A Distant Temple

They brought him to Jerusalem, to present him to the Lord;
...And to offer a sacrifice according to that which is said in the
law of the Lord. Luke 2:22–24

Day by day the bureaucratic process of the census grinds on.
Gradually the crowds thin out as individuals and families,
their obligation to Roman authority met, leave to return home.
Now it is possible to look for shelter, to find perhaps the house
of a friend or distant relation.

This isn't ideal for any woman. Yet it is a solution to the
problem of having to journey north again so soon after the
child's birth. Her young body will heal; yet the heat, the jog-
ging of the beast, the constant anxiety of the journey —
everything points to waiting, both for her sake and for the
child's. If necessary, Joseph's skills are marketable. So they
wait and rest. There is another reason. The visit to the rabbi is
only the first of two things they are bound to do for their child.

She looked at him and shuddered as the thought of a long ago
custom came to her. Among these very hills a thousand years
before (some whispered that it was even in more recent centuries), the first-born child was doomed to be offered as a
sacrifice. Nowadays a simple ceremony recalled that ancient
barbaric custom. To carry out the observation demanded by
the law, they would take the child to a priest to present him to
the Lord; then they would receive him back at the priest's
hands. Now that they were here in Judea, they could take him
to the very heart of their world, the great temple only a few
miles away in Jerusalem.

For Mary and Joseph coming from Bethlehem through
Bethany, seeing the city as they came over the shoulder of the
Mount of Olives, the temple must have been a breath-taking
sight. It was new, finished only a few years before by Herod's
work force. Six city blocks long, it swept across their view
from north to south, dazzlingly white under the blue sky, its
southern pinnacle a hundred and twenty feet above the drop
into the valley below. From east and west converged a system
of soaring aquaducts that supplied it with water. At the north
end the sanctuary itself rose up from the area of courtyards. It

stood above the hills, higher than the largest of the great Gothic cathedrals which would one day stand above generations to come.

For Mary and Joseph, looking down from high above the Kidron Valley east of the city, there must have been almost inexpressible fulfillment in this moment. They were gazing at what, in the deepest sense, was their spiritual home. If in that journey they chose also to make this resting point a moment to feed her child, she may well have sung softly to him the timeless words composed for this very moment and for this very prospect.

The Lord himself is thy keeper:
The Lord is thy defence upon thy right hand;
so that the sun shall not burn thee by day,
neither the moon by night.

As she sang, she held in her arms him who was to challenge and question all that she and Joseph saw before them. The temple embodied law, authority, ritual, traditon, institution — all these things existing to be a vehicle to something beyond each of them. Then and in every age and every culture, they exist to make possible a living dialogue between God and humanity. In every age they need the goad of prophecy and the inspiration of the spirit to prevent their becoming ends in themselves. In Mary's arms lay both the goad and the inspiration. The struggle between inspiration and institution, authority and freedom, tradition and innovation is fought with passion and without mercy. Both forces see themselves as the instruments of God.

This particular chapter of that struggle sees the temple on the hill called Moriah facing a cross on a nearby hill called Golgotha. But the tension is universal in human affairs and unending in human history. There will always be the temple and the cross. Always in a thousand Jerusalems across time and the world die the ten thousand prophets who come with the vision renewed and energized. Always in an enduring and tragic irony, the temples of every century, by their crucifixions, make possible within themselves the resurrections which ensure that the visions change and transform those who reject them!

The Threat of a Sword

And, behold, there was a man in Jerusalem, whose name was Simeon; ...and he came by the Spirit into the temple: and when the parents brought in the child Jesus, to do for him after the custom of the law, Then took he him up in his arms.

Luke 2:25-28

They had reached the safe anonymity of the temple area, joining the great tide of humanity that day after day moved up and down the vast steps and across the succession of court-yards toward the sacrificial area. They purchased the birds which they would offer in place of their child. Traditionally they were buying him back, redeeming him from God whose he was. One day near this same temple there would be no birds to purchase, no alternative to the utter and terrible self-sacrifice by which he would give himself. But for now the inex-pensive birds, all that they could afford, were handed to the priest and the sacrifice was performed. To fulfill the law was joy and fulfillment.

Even what happened immediately afterward was a matter for smiles and tenderness. The temple was a centre for every aspect of life. Around it wandered some elderly men and women, deeply devout, dreaming the dreams of old age, accepted, understood, and respected by the passing crowds. Two of them had come, attracted as we often are in our elderly years to the beauty of infancy and young parenthood. Everyone knew them. They were part of the familiar scene of the temple.

It was only when the old man took her child and walked a little away from them that she became alarmed. It was more than the natural concern about his steadiness. The child seemed to move the old man to deep emotion. The weak voice gathered strength. Rocking the child a little, the elderly feet began to move in the shuffle of a half forgotten dance. Then the words came, and as they did a most extraordinary thing took place. This bent old man, seemingly insignificant in this place of power and wealth, seemed to grow. He began quietly, almost whispering, but then his ringing words swept out and beyond the temple, out over the city, beyond even the com-munities of Israel scattered across the known world. "Salvation," he sang, "salvation before the face of all people." Lifting the child even higher the vast world of his imagination seemed revealed to him. "A light," he shouted, "a light to lighten the Gentiles, and to be the glory of thy people Israel."

Here again for Mary was the mingling of promise and threat. She had felt it in the very air the night that her child was born, heard it in the uncomprehending chatter of the shepherds. It was hinted in the angelic annunciation she had received. Always there was the implication that her child belonged not to her but to some far and vast world, a world that her mind failed to envision, and so relapsed into uncomprehending dread.

Her child was again in her arms. Joseph and she said the effusive things that sometimes suffice to extract us from situations that threaten to get out of hand. They prepared to leave, grateful that the episode was over. They were only a few paces away when they heard the old man's voice. It was low, hesitating, almost as if he was speaking against his own will. His dimming eyes were fixed on her alone. The child, Joseph — all else seemed not to exist. His voice was very tender, almost as if he wished to mitigate the terrible words as much as possible. "You," he said to her, "you shall be pierced to the heart." As soon as he had said it, he turned quickly and moved away into the crowd which had gathered to watch and listen.

Before Simeon has disappeared into the crowds of time he has spoken to everyone of us. He has voiced something all the more terrible because it is voiced about love, that elusive treasure we all long for. Simeon shows us that all love is experienced in the shadow of the sword. Perhaps even more terrible is the fact that renouncing love does not free us from the sword. For if the price of loving somebody is the certainty of the eventual loss of that person, the price of refusing to love is the loss of our capacity to love and be loved. Thus, attempting to escape a sword, we are pierced by an even more terrible one.

For Mary it may well have been the last straw. She had come to this place for celebration, but now ran from it in terror. She held her child closely, every muscle in her body straining to protect him against the threatening nightmares suddenly unleashed in her imagination.

The Dark Fortress

Now when Jesus was born in Bethlehem of Judea in the days of Herod the king, behold, there came wise men from the east to Jerusalem. Matthew 2:1

The intimacy and peace of Bethlehem were balm to the emotional wounds of the Jerusalem journey. There was the intense pleasure of her child—the tangible joys of handling his body, the thousand meaningless syllables of love exchanged between them. All these pleasures moved her toward healing and peace as day followed day.

By now she and Joseph were planning their return north to Nazareth. They had tentatively arranged to join a group soon leaving. Very soon they would move out of the town and over the open fields to the road winding down thousands of feet to the throbbing heat of the Jordan valley. As they left Bethlehem and headed east, they would move slowly under the shadow of the Herodium. The Herodium was only one link in a massive and interlocked chain of forts ranging from south of the Dead Sea to Galilee. Yet even as this young woman, her child in her arms, looked across at the dark citadel from the village on the hill, it may have occurred to her that such power resided in the capacity to terminate life rather than to initiate it.

In the inner geography which we all inhabit, we encounter fortifications of our own construction. Walls and battlements of fear, anxiety, alienation, depression, stand to keep out what we see as enemy. Ironically our enemies can very often bring about our changing, our freedom, and our growth. As aging, internal tyrants they stand within us, determined to crush the child of possibility trying to come to birth in each of us.

Mary could not know it, but even as she made her eager preparation for the journey home, another far longer journey was ending. A few miles away from her a group of travellers had arrived at the huge gate blocking the winding ramp to the top of the Herodium far above. They had asked for an audience with Herod, then in residence. It had been granted. The old king, ravaged by responsibility, age, debauchery, disease, faced the distinguished Persians. Herod knew they represented an empire that even mighty Rome always regarded carefully in its dealings. The long social obligations of desert hospitality were observed before their purpose was revealed. As they began to explain, Herod showed no outward sign of his feelings.

What the Persians described would have been perfectly visible to Mary as she walked under a late evening sky. But unlike them she would not have known what the skies were saying. Herod looked at the star charts that the visitors spread for him. "If the king would wish to come outside on the ramparts...?" But the offer was refused. The pain-racked body, once athletic and distinguished, was unable to comply. But the evidence was there in the charts. Jupiter and Saturn were again in conjunction in the constellation of Pisces. When last the heavens had shown such a pattern, the voice of Isaiah, now nearly eight centuries silent, had echoed in these fields and hills.

Jupiter, explained the quiet intellectual voice of the visitor, was the ruler of the heavens. Saturn was the planet of Palestine. Pisces symbolized an age of change, turmoil, crisis, decision. Facing the seated Herod, the Persian posed the question which would have such terrible consequences. "Where," asked the visitor of his host, "where is the child who is born to be king of the Jews?"

This question, asked long ago in a particular situation, is of course universal and timeless. The travelling philosopher who asked it inhabits each of us, whether or not we are aware of him behind our external busyness. The question we ask concerns the whereabouts of the child who is somewhere in the tangled and troubled terrain of our own souls and personalities. The child we seek is, in history and in time, the Christ; but in our personal experience he is the light of God, always struggling for birth within us. "Where is the child?" we ask the kings and tyrants of self-centredness, cynicism, and weariness that rule our inmost hearts. And we ask for this child because we are instinctively aware that if only we can find him, we will discover a king who will draw us and lead us to new life.

"Where?" asked the patient voice again, "where is the child who is born to be king...?"

A Coming of Kings

When they had heard the king, they departed; and, lo, the star,
which they saw in the east, went before them, till it came and
stood over where the young child was.   Matthew 2:9

The star systems wheel endlessly across the galaxies. They do
not stop, much less do they stop over particular houses. But
human journeys stop, and in our human travelling we know
when we have come to the place where our star has been
leading us.

High on the plateaux of Persia the courts of Zoroaster and his
religion had devised over the centuries their own complex
logic for perceiving order and meaning in human affairs by
linking them with the movements of the stars. They knew
that this extraordinary conjunction of Jupiter and Saturn in the
constellation called Pisces, coming as it did only once in
almost eight hundred years, pointed to Palestine for its meaning. Now, as they stood in front of this Idumean monarch
named Herod, watching with hidden amusement the conster-
nation caused by their question about the birth of a child, they
knew that they had not gone astray. And when the whispering
of the king and his advisors died down, and they heard a cour-
tier read from one of the scrolls mentioning the name of
Bethlehem, they knew that for them the star-travelling had
ended.

There followed the studied and extended pleasantries of
Eastern hospitality—questions about their huge and distant
homeland, polite interest in their astrology and astronomy.
When they left, they received the formal invitation to return.
With equal formality, they promised to do so. As they left the
Herodium, working their way down the hillside ramp, they
were extremely careful to notice pursuit or observation. They
took similar care in their inquiries in the following days.

Discreetly and efficiently they filtered pieces of information.
Their ancient wisdom made them open to the humour of a God
who betrayed his presence in ways easy to ignore. Princes who
walked among men as beggars were the stock-in-trade of their
legends. So they asked again about the family who had occupied the now vacant cave at the time of the census taking.

There was something about that situation, they thought, that suggested a possible divine subtlety and irony.

God is one who most often enters the stage of our experience by a side entrance. We become aware that while we were involved in the action in centre stage, God has entered almost unnoticed. There is often an ordinariness in his way of entering. We know some of his disguises. There are the deceptive simplicities of bread and wine and water, or the child, or the madonna holding her child. These we have learned. But God can adopt a myriad disguises—a phone call, a casual remark, a relationship, a sickness. There is no end to the divine disguise. As the Magi well knew, it could even be a disguise as normal and predictable as a pattern of stars! And because they were wise men, they looked for what others had already dismissed as ordinary and of no particular consequence.

When they came to the house, they knew that the star charts had not lied. Here, recognized by wisdom and by instinct, the lines met to form intersections, meetings of human life and heavenly motion, of divine purpose and human obedience, of time and eternity, of spirit and flesh, of God's wisdom and a child's crying. They looked into the eyes of a woman who was virgin and mother, peasant and queen. They knelt on the rough serrated stone of the floor.

Before her in the small room, the silent self-assured visitors placed their gifts. They were tiny and seemingly insignificant, as are often gifts that bear scrutiny for their immense value alone. She dutifully held them before her child's eyes, watching him focus for a moment, as any child would, on the sheen and the colour, felt him reach out to touch and then quickly withdraw. She noticed with wonder the tiny flame of the oil lamp reflected in burnished gold. She sensed a precious ointment in its container, expensive, sweet-smelling, remote from her experience.

Ever after, when she remembered that day, she wondered if she and the child had not encountered angels. She knew that angels had a way of appearing in many guises to speak to mortals. Yet always the gold and the frankincense and the myrrh remained as mute witness to the fact that the vast and jealous world had come to claim him. In the future, unavoidable and unpredictable, it lay waiting.

A Dream of Death

Behold, the angel of the Lord appeareth to Joseph in a dream, saying, Arise, and take the young child and his mother, and flee into Egypt.   Matthew 2:13

Life in Judea was lived on the edge of danger. Personal and family life, especially at the lower levels of the social scale, were always threatened by the political forces that fought out the constant struggle for real or apparent power. A tyrant's whim could bring overnight impoverishment, banishment, never ending imprisonment, instant death. Political involvement, activity which linked a man to the many radical movements in the area, was a luxury for the young, the totally committed, or those who had suffered so much that revenge had become an obsession that gave meaning to their lives.

For most of us in western society the situation is very far from our experience. We take for granted the rightness of the law's process, the accountability of powers in society, the measure of freedom and safety in which we live. Even the exceptions, the times when such things are challenged, or betrayed by violence or injustice, are themselves pointers to the existence of our securities and freedoms. So true is this that we can forget the existence of societies inhabited by millions of contemporary Josephs, vulnerable to tyranny, possessing no security, having recourse to no defences, sometimes dispossessed, and sometimes even physically tortured. We have many unknown brothers whose name and nightmare is that of Joseph.

He was well aware that the visitors had singled them out in the town's life. He may well have deeply regretted bringing the family back to Bethlehem from the temple visit, rather than heading north for Galilee and home. But the damage was done. He knew too the danger of the expensive gifts. He may have warned Mary about showing them or even mentioning that they existed. His blood ran cold as he realized the misinterpretations that could be placed on those gifts. He could imagine the treatment he would receive to persuade him to admit that he had traded information to foreigners.

They should go quickly. At least that was definite. They had been on the verge of going anyway; so she would not be distressed. From the beginning she had known that their stay in Bethlehem was temporary. But was it safe to head for Galilee? It would take them more than two days to get out of Judea. But this was the direction that others would presume they had gone. Should there be questions asked, this was the direction their pursuers would go.

Suddenly he knew what he had to do. It was as if a voice had spoken, resolving conflict, lighting a clear way, transforming dreams into a reality that could be dealt with. They would go to Egypt. He woke her and told her what he feared. In their blood through countless generations sounded the screams of children, butchered in unnumbered battles and invasions, purges and frenzies.

Such frenzy a paranoid mind was even then expressing in shouted orders in the mountain fortress five miles away. Word had come that the Persians had been seen crossing the Jordan eastward and heading into the desert. The hooves thundered down the ramp, dark shadows separating at the mountain's base to approach the nearby town from different directions. The early bird songs were drowned by rising screams, the dawn light on the hills gave way to deeper scarlet. Death came to Bethlehem as the dark angel had once come to the houses of the Egyptians on that Passover night of ancient terror. But now blood sprinkled on a door meant not a sparing but the slaughter of a child.

When the door crashed down before the onslaught, the family was already on the edge of the desert, exchanging certain death for a possible death. If they reached Egypt, they could safely lose themselves in the teeming streets of Alexandria. Among its million Jews there would be resources for a refugee family. Ideally there would eventually be work for Joseph. Above all the child was safe.

The image of the three of them is for Christians a thing of long tradition. Joseph and Mary and the child move toward Egypt across the leaded barriers of unnumbered stained glass windows. But of course, as we worship in their coloured light, a million families flee across a score of distant frontiers where Mary and the Christ child looked daily on terror, through eyes that are African or Asian or South American.

To Be a Pilgrim

O how lovely are thy dwellings, thou Lord of hosts! My soul hath a desire and longing to enter into the courts of the Lord: my heart and my flesh rejoice in the living God. Yea, the sparrow hath found her an house, and the swallow a nest where she may lay her young.   Psalm 84:1–3

He was now twelve—interesting, intelligent, growing. She had been looking forward to this year. The Passover feast was of course celebrated in Nazareth, as in every community and indeed every home, but nothing was quite the same as experiencing a time of religious festival in Jerusalem itself.

Jerusalem was a great part of the mystique. It called to one all life long. Its towers haunted the imagination. It had become the subject of innumerable songs. Across trackless deserts, in foreign cities, from ships on the Mediterranean and on the Persian Gulf, from the valleys of Gaul and the western empire, Jerusalem called men and women home to her narrow crowded streets. In comparison to her age and history Rome and Athens were upstarts. At the heart of Jerusalem stood the temple. Beside it the shrines and temples of the empire paled into insignificance. Herod, who knew the empire from Rome in the west to Petra in the east, had seen to that.

Mary and Joseph and their son would not go to Jerusalem as mere travellers to see the sights. They would go as pilgrims to worship. This year, for the first time since his infancy, they would bring their son. Perhaps, she thought whimsically, they could show him to old Simeon if he was still haunting the building. She knew too that for Joseph it would be an experience of great pride to bring the boy. There might not be too many opportunities in the future. Even if Joseph had a long life ahead of him, he was not getting any younger, and the journey made great demands on strong legs and good lungs.

She couldn't help but reflect on how time itself was two-edged. The very passing of time, which allows us to celebrate the growing and maturing of a child into adulthood, is the same measure of our own aging. Fulfillment mingles with fear, anticipation with regret, growth with anticipated diminishment. She knew too that her son was ripe for this visit. The early years were gone when she could enter into his thinking, when she could be allowed to share his dreams and reflections. But she knew that they were there, in the silences, behind his eyes, in the sometimes distant voice of a reply or a question asked.

She was learning to let go. It wasn't easy. Before her eyes a child was dying and changing, and becoming a youth. The dying and rising in that process is both painful and beautiful for all the actors in the universal, yet always unique, human drama. She was aware of a great trust, which she found hard to define yet of which she was quite sure. Sometimes the responsibility of this covenant made with the future, a covenant known by every sensitive parent, feels almost too heavy to bear.

She realized too that, as he was her first-born, she had to learn of a boy's growth through him. Learning to be a parent was a strain—choosing to speak or not to speak, to question or not to question, to guide or to stand back and watch while a hard lesson is learned from experience. All these were now part of her daily life. She often thought of Simeon and his word about a sword. She may sometimes have thought that what Simeon said was true of all parents and children. As in all relationships there had been many moments of minor pain, misunderstandings, disobediences. But so far, no terrors. Humanly she allowed her mind to slide away from following her own thoughts into areas she didn't wish to enter. If there were to be elements ahead that she had to face, then so be it. There was little point in robbing the present moment of its happiness.

She found herself smiling. After all, Joseph was well. They were proud of this boy on the edge of young manhood. She herself was in her prime. They would go to Jerusalem.

A Journey in Joy

And the child grew, and waxed strong in spirit, filled with wisdom: and the grace of God was upon him. Now his parents went to Jerusalem every year at the feast of the passover. And when he was twelve years old, they went up to Jerusalem after the custom of the feast.   Luke 2:40–42

During Passover season there would be no difficulty finding a group they could travel with. As always they would have to take the roundabout route down through the Jordan valley, the route that ended in the ghastly climb up the hills toward Jerusalem. The much shorter route lead down from Nazareth to the valley below, over the rich fertile earth of its fields, across the great international caravan route, which itself went on west to the coast, south through Samaria, and along the backbone of the high country of northern Judea to Jerusalem. Those who had made the journey spoke of the attractiveness of Samaria—the road winding through valleys, their floors rich with crops, the mountainsides covered with olive trees. But history came between travellers and the roads of Samaria. For centuries there had been enmity. Some hardy souls did from time to time risk going straight south, taking with them sufficient food and hired servants who doubled as body-guards. But otherwise it was too risky.

She moved through the days of preparation, making sure that things were ready, left tidy, cleaned. Joseph put in extra hours completing needed orders. Sometimes she would glance anxiously at Joseph, knowing that much of the future depended on his ability to work.

Groups formed near the well in the centre of town. From there, having counted heads, tightened straps, said goodbyes to family, taken last minute messages to be passed on, they moved through the town and headed southeast. Late in the afternoon they rounded the foot of Mount Tabor, and the country began to slope away toward the river valley. Below and beyond they could see other groups of travellers heading like themselves for Jerusalem.

The next few days were punctuated by the rhythms of the journey. Preparing the simple meals, bedding down in the outer courtyard of an inn, pointing out various things to her son on the rare occasions when he left the other youngsters to speak to them, chatting to Joseph when he was not with the men, finding a moment to go with the other women to a stream or to the river itself to wash a garment and give it time to dry in the sun.

The road was absolutely familiar to her. Year by year they had taken it since their marriage. She found herself recalling her first emotion laden sight of this valley when she had first travelled it on her visit to Elizabeth. Its walls seemed to hem her in, bringing back the imprisoned feeling of that long ago pregnancy, the feeling of being taken over, locked into a task and a destiny which allowed no escape and accepted no refusal. For the most part this sensation had left her as the baby grew to childhood and on to healthy energetic youth. There were moments when she could almost have believed that the experience beginning it all had been a dream.

For each of us there are certain places where we invest much of our living. As for Mary, so sometimes with us, it may be an actual road or stretch of highway travelled and retravelled in different stages and for different reasons. It may be a cottage shared at different stages of a family's life. But each becomes something more than an external reference point. Each becomes an interior place, an inner highway, and each leads us to discover and rediscover different levels of ourselves.

Somewhere ahead of her a voice began to sing. It was one of the young people beginning one of the travelling songs he would have learnt in the synagogue school.

When the Lord restored the fortunes of Zion,
then were we like unto them that dream.
Then was our mouth filled with laughter
and our tongue with joy.
Then said they among the nations,
The Lord hath done great things for them.

From where she stood she could see her son joining in the song. The Lord had indeed done great things for her. She had sown in tears and, at least for this lovely moment of freedom, she was reaping in joy. Tomorrow by nightfall they would hear the eastern city gate of Jerusalem close behind them.

A Night of Fear

And when they had fulfilled the days, as they returned, the child Jesus tarried behind in Jerusalem; and Joseph and his mother knew not of it. But they, supposing him to have been in the company, went a day's journey; and they sought him among their kinsfolk and acquaintance. And when they found him not, they turned back again to Jerusalem. Luke 2:43–45

The experience was beyond her expectations. She had known that he would be interested. She had not realized how much. Every aspect of the pulsing life of the temple fascinated him. Time and time again they had to bring his eager youthful questioning of officials to an end, apologizing for their son's insatiable curiosity.

Their own Passover, eaten with friends, was likewise intensely moving. The boy seemed to have a deep commitment to every nuance of the long timeless ceremony. Nothing escaped his mind as it searched for meaning in the simplest things. What did the herbs mean? What were the traditions attached to the lamb? What were the passages of scripture being read? Jerusalem was a feast in itself for him. He rubbed shoulders with the world in the teeming narrow streets. Roman soldiers he had seen many times. But here were Roman civil servants, Greek actors, business men from Alexandria and Antioch, exotic foreigners from Ephesus, Persians whose sophistication made it difficult to believe that they shared a tradition with simple Galileans.

Now it was over, and Jerusalem was behind them for at least another year. To some extent, she thought, it would now depend on Joseph whether they would come this way again as a family. Because of its hilltop setting, the city stayed within sight for most of their first morning's travel. When finally the last glittering pinnacle of the walls disappeared behind a hill, she felt a sense of profound sadness, as if something had ended beyond the mere feast season itself.

She wondered if this feeling sprang from the changes in her son. She found herself thinking of him now no longer as a child. Even in these few days she had noticed a difference, had seen a sense of the larger world being born in his eyes, in the excitement of his voice, in his increasing wish to move from her and from Joseph into the company of other youths, or even on occasion to be obviously wishing for solitude. She smiled as she remembered how her own parents often had remarked on her readiness to turn deeply into herself, to think about things said, events seen, to let them sink deep down until their meaning became clear and she could speak of them again.

It would soon be time to stop for the evening meal. She had noticed Joseph from time to time involved with the other men. It was only when they came together and asked each other the same question—on the lips of every parent some time or other — that the first tinge of disquiet came. At first, a little annoyed, they inquired among the other families, all of them settling down for the evening. Always the answer was the same. Nobody had noticed him. In fact one of the youngsters said they hadn't seen him all day. This changed everything. Her instinct was to turn back and begin the climb up to Jerusalem immediately. As Joseph pointed out the impossibility of this, she knew he was right. The road from Jerusalem to Jericho was notorious. They would simply have to wait till morning.

She prepared a supper that she herself could not eat. For a while they were joined by friends who said all the helpful things friends say at such times. She felt that sleep might make the morning come more quickly, but no sleep came. She lay in the mingled lights and shadows of the low fire and the distant stars, her mind assailed by possibilities. She thought of other starlit nights when kings had visited him as a child. She thought again of the sword that the old man had mentioned. Any fear, any anxiety drew it from the scabbord of her unconscious. She lay, as we all have lain and will again, listening to the night world, joining its sounds and shadows with her own inner fears until together they brought terror.

Before the dawn Joseph woke her from a short sleep of exhaustion. They should leave before the heat of the day.

His Father's Business

His mother said unto him, Son, why hast thou thus dealt with us? behold, thy father and I have sought thee sorrowing. And he said unto them, How is it that ye sought me? wist ye not that I must be about my Father's business? And they understood not the saying which he spake unto them.

Luke 2:48–50

A harsh sun sweeping in across the desert found them well on their way. During the day it would be reasonably safe because they would constantly encounter others returning home. All morning their eyes searched the road ahead, scanning the figures even before faces became recognizable. Every disappointment drained more of their energy. On their own they had moved more quickly than in the caravan. Late afternoon found them entering the shadows of the gate and having to decide where to search in the labyrinth of streets. Each thought of a possibility proved wrong. By now the sun was going down once again, the streets were emptying. It was Joseph who forced her to stop, saw that she ate a little, found them a shelter for her second sleepless night.

It was at the top of the great staircase to the temple area that fear and exhaustion nearly overcame her. She knew that Joseph too was nearly at the end of his resources. Even after the feast the place was thronged. It was while they were searching for some quiet spot to gather their energies that they heard the voices, the unmistakable high excited babble of scholars in disputation. It was a sight they had often seen but never felt themselves to be part of. Their world was simpler and more practical. They were not privy to these never-ending subtleties, this rarefied language, this endless scoring of points.

When the gesticulating figures parted for a moment, she saw her son's face. What shocked her more than anything was the change in it. The scholarly gesturing of the hand, the seriousness, the intensity, the self-assurance that was not arrogance. The thought came to her that, far from being lost, he was in some extraordinary way totally at home. For a moment she and Joseph stood feeling the situation to be so different from their anticipation of it. Somewhere, she had presumed, she would find him, call to him, see his delight and relief, and there would be joyful if questioning reunion. That, she realized, had been her mental picture. But this was utterly different. In fact, the final straw came as they stood transfixed. It seemed to her that his eyes caught hers, recognized her, but did not interrupt the dialogue in which he was engaged.

This broke her stillness. She and Joseph moved through the group. She could hardly wait for a lull in the discussion. All her pent up worry and tiredness was in the cry, "Why have you treated us like this?"

From a long distance his eyes returned to focus on hers. When he spoke, she felt for a moment that even his voice had changed. There is nothing more startling than to discern, at the heart of the familiar, a new and unknown quantity. "Did you not know," he said very quietly, "that I was bound to be in my Father's house."

Parental love is hostage to its child. A parent always carries a measure of guilt, a sense of partial failure, a constant and familiar list of things done and not done. All it takes from the child is a sentence to bring all this guilt and failure, or at least the sense of it, to the surface. In response there sweeps over our insecure parenthood a whole welter of emotions, among them guilt, resentment, anger, helplessness. We are appalled that all our efforts to understand are dismissed as misunderstanding. We are deeply hurt, all the more so because the source of the criticism, however gentle, makes it seem harsh and wounding.

Long afterwards she had vague memories of well meaning compliments being given by unknown voices and faces. Her first instinct was to get away, to take him with them. She thought about this many times in the following days as they covered the miles northward. She dreamt one night that she was struggling with a great dragon. The nightmare beast was tearing her child from her. She awoke in tears, not knowing whether she could have won the struggle had it not ended in her waking.

A Pondering Heart

He went down with them, and came to Nazareth, and was subject unto them: but his mother kept all these sayings in her heart. And Jesus increased in wisdom and stature, and in favour with God and man. Luke 2:51–52

Sometimes in the summertime, when there was respite from the normal daily work which had to be done, she would rest a little in the shelter of cool green branches which they had built over the flat roof. Life was peaceful. It moved to the rhythms of the countryside. Ancient clocks, unseen and immeasurably old, counted out the life of her home and her village. She still liked to go to the well, a meeting place with friends, never seeing the water ripple from her water-pot without remembering the Presence felt there years ago.

They had not gone to Jerusalem since that still vividly remembered and deeply felt episode. Somehow each time they had found a legitimate reason for not going. One year it was too dangerous because of the insurrection and Roman military response. Another year money was scarce. Yet another year there was sickness. But she sometimes wondered if there wasn't a deeper reason, a remembering of too much fear, too much pain.

Below her she could hear the sounds of life in the house. The main part of the home was a single room built on the side of the hill. The roof was flat. A stair ran up the outside where she was sitting. The single room doubled as a shop and workroom by day, and a bedroom by night. At times the flat roof was a quiet place to lie looking up at the stars and waiting for sleep.

Those days Joseph had as much work as he could do. The economy was good. The estates and small farms that covered most of Galilee always needed farm implements. The army always needed axles, wheels, cages for prisoners, sometimes crosses. It was really a question of how much energy he had, although he was helped now by another set of hands. Joseph took pleasure in passing on his skill to a son who was becoming a young man.

But she knew, as did Joseph, that her son's thoughts were not primarily on carpentry. He never betrayed impatience or disinterest. Yet there was a holding back of interest and energy for other things. Once when he was a child, Mary had taken him to listen to Hillel, the greatest of rabbis. Hillel had died when the boy was ten. Yet something had radiated from the elderly man, something of the beauty and gentleness of his spirit. She could sometimes hear her son talking about Hillel's thoughts and sayings with others of his age. Even though most of his schooling had been in the synagogue, she knew that her son spent a great deal of time with the rabbi, endlessly discussing, avidly reading, forever questioning.

Sometimes she found herself praying for him. She felt instinctively that something was beginning to call, something infinitely far yet near beyond description. She recalled this feeling from years before. She had known it in the Presence that had announced his birth. She had felt it when the Persian travellers had come with the gifts that she still treasured. There had always been a sense of sharing her son with distant looming powers and destinies, whose presence she felt but whose form and source she could never quite define. Sometimes the poetry of Isaiah would come to her mind, lines learnt in her own childhood.

Unto us a child is born
unto us a son is given.

In these two lines from long ago was stated the simple, understandable fact she knew so well. For her the coming of the child and son had been utter joy. But she could not help recalling that the long ago singer had also said,

The government shall be upon his shoulder;
his name shall be called wonderful, counsellor.

In these lines came the great clouds mysteriously clustered around the simplicty of the first statement. It seemed to her as if similar clouds were gathering around the simplicities of motherhood and childhood, of love and growing and relationship. Why, she wondered, is joy in adult life never total, but always shadowed by clouds passing across the landscape of one's mind.

Coming to Terms

When I was a child, I spake as a child, I understood as a child, I thought as a child: but when I became a man, I put away childish things. For now we see through a glass, darkly; but then face to face: now I know in part; but then shall I know even as also I am known. 1 Corinthians 13:11-12

With the passing of time, the reference points of life change. She realized it one day as she watched her son chatting with his cousin James.

Until Joseph's death, time for both of them had flowed from the boy, from that long ago sense of a Presence, from the birth itself, from the deep sense of mystery, even if a frightening mystery, that all of these memories had engendered. But now that Joseph was gone, something had changed. He had been away from home a great deal. As any journeyman carpenter, he had had to take contracts where and when they came. She recalled the excitement of the news that Herod Antipas was commissioning a huge building project at Sepphoris only three miles from Nazareth. She little knew that her husband's body would be returned to her after a construction accident.

Those were the years when the family had rallied round. She and Joseph had always been close to her brother Clopas and his wife, also called Mary. They had a large family, seven in all, four boys and three girls, and all his life her son had been accepted among them almost like another brother. She had always been grateful for that.

More and more she found herself thinking of Joseph these days, of their years together. They had not been easy years. Their early hopes for a settled life, for building a home in Nazareth, had been shattered by the necessity to take that desperate escape to Egypt, to survive there on very little. Even on their return they had been made to realize that they could never show their faces near Bethlehem again, after what had happened. Families had been bereaved because of her child. She had no need to search for signs of the sword promised by old Simeon.

Even in her own relationship with her son there were fears and anxieties. He had never betrayed her of course. He was even now carrying on what Joseph had been doing. Yet she knew that his heart wasn't in it. She knew too that even in the circle of the family there were feelings that somehow created distance and unsureness. To Clopas, his uncle, he was almost a son, to the other children, almost a brother. She smiled as she remembered that they were all in their twenties now, Jesus himself one of the older ones with James and Joses. And yet even among them there were times when he seemed—what words could she use—far off, different, detached.

She felt too her own vulnerability. It wasn't an easy society for a widow. People were thoughtful of course, but once widowed you became somehow less substantial, a kind of ghost, ageless, insignificant, accepted in some ways, yet in others passed by and ignored. Financially she was now totally dependent on this man, once her child, now a restless, reflective, unknown quality in her home. She knew with a certainty she could not explain that she would attend no wedding feast for him. Yet beyond this there was no clear idea of the future emerging. Even if he did leave her one day, she knew she was more fortunate than most. She would always be accepted into Clopas' household.

Still chatting, the two men had moved outside. She felt a vague unease that the gesture shut her out of some other world. Part of her knew that she had to respect his adulthood now, but still there was resentment. She would always recall looking into his twelve year old eyes in the temple courtyard, and finding that she was outside of something. How ironic it was that in one sense he was totally hers, her child, yet in another and increasing sense he was not hers at all. When he came in, neither of them spoke.

A First Farewell

The voice of one crying in the wilderness, Prepare ye the way of the Lord, make his paths straight. John did baptize in the wilderness....And it came to pass in those days, that Jesus came from Nazareth of Galilee, and was baptized of John in Jordan.
Mark 1:3-9

She was weeping and at the same time angry at herself for weeping. Between her sobs she could feel the tides of anger and resentment sweeping over her. It was a diffuse, unspecified anger, and it took in the whole world and all of life, as such anger does. He had gone. He would of course return. She knew that. He had promised he would. But she also knew that in a deeper sense the man who had left would not return. Life itself would not return to what it had been. And since she knew that this iron law of time governs all relationships, all families, all of life, she accepted it and yet wept in the face of its inevitability.

She wept angrily at the world as it had become. Why could it not be peaceful, settled, unified? As she grew older and more desirous of peace, there seemed to be even less peace on all sides. The country was in constant restlessness. Hardly a week went by without trouble. Either the troops of Herod or the local Roman detachment would be pursuing rebels in the hills. The days were alive with rumour, resentment, fear. She knew that some young men of the village had mysteriously disappeared into the hill country across the lake. They called them zealots, and the Romans feared them enough to be merciless when they captured them. She had once seen a group of crosses erected at a roadside, and she and others had hastily detoured to return another way to the village.

At least, thank God, he had not decided to take that option. He had come to her with news of Elizabeth's John, now creating quite a stir in the southern Jordan valley. He had told her that he was convinced he had to go to see John, and he knew that she would understand. He wasn't the only one going. He had heard that some of the young men from Capernaum were also going down. The fact that he was heading south gave some reassurance to her, although the political and religious atmosphere was so volatile that she still found herself imagining possibilities that filled her with fear.

She had heard of the movement which John had joined. Nazarites, they were called. She sometimes wondered if the harsh desert beyond the river drove them a little mad. Elizabeth and Zachariah had not lived to see their son shouting at the curious faithful crowds who came out of Jericho, and even from Jerusalem, to listen to his cutting condemnations of their society, their politics, their life-styles. Maybe it was a sick world, yet she didn't want that ranting alienated role for her son. Crowds were strange, fickle, terrible. Always hanging around the edge were spears and spies and troublemakers.

She wondered if he would go further south to Qumran. She wouldn't be surprised if the community attracted him. They always welcomed skills. He would fit in, she thought, to the rhythm of the community. Essenes, they called them. They too had written off society as terminally ill, and had moved away to the vivid searing light and heat and silence of the Dead Sea area. If she had to lose him to something, she hoped it would be to that. At least there he would be out of danger, and perhaps he would bring to birth something of beauty and value that would spread and affect the country.

Because life is both an interior and exterior journey, we constantly transfer from one to the other, using each as an arena for our feelings. Fear of the unknown, fear of change, a sense of betrayal or loss or failure—all can be transferred into anger at the outside world. Our struggling to find faith can make us angry at the church. Fear about health can create a deep resentment of everything medical. Not being able to cope with our job can bring deep hatred of the firm, the government, society in general. All is bitterness, all horizons are dark, all friendship is suspect. The shadow of our own little inner citadel swells into an enormous cloud enveloping the whole world.

She found herself again, as she had done so often, going back to the moment of the Presence and its annunciation. It had all sounded so vast and magnificent. Yet where was it all now? What had it all meant? The world was still the same. The mighty were still in their seats. Her spirit no longer rejoiced in God. Yet even the thought brought guilt sweeping over her, and she wept.

The Coming of Strangers

Jesus, walking by the sea of Galilee, saw two brethren, Simon called Peter, and Andrew his brother, casting a net into the sea: for they were fishers. And he saith unto them, Follow me, and I will make you fishers of men. And they straightway left their nets, and followed him. Matthew 4:18–20

He was never coming back. She had known this for some weeks. Others had come back from the Jordan area, and from them she had learned what had happened. At least she had learned what they had witnessed. She herself could guess what had happened within him. And because she knew intuitively, she knew with a terrible certainty that nothing would ever be the same again.

Waves of feeling swept over her. She felt fear, a fear for him and for herself. Fear brought anger, anger that he hadn't told her of this. And yet she realized that he couldn't possibly have told her, because he himself had to go to discover whatever it was. But the anger swept over her and included all the silences between them, all the feeling of being on the outside of him looking in, all the anticipating of she knew not what. The long ago statements made about him, made in that far away moment which changed her life forever, hung now unresolved, unfulfilled, becoming threats to be feared rather than hopes to be kept alive.

Suddenly she felt a terrible resentment about it all. She resented a god who chose people with promises and hopes that turned into frustration and unrelenting drudgery. She identified with the shadowy figures in stories she had heard so many times as a child, when the old rabbi read the scrolls. Moses raging against a grudging people, Jeremiah desperately pleading to be heard. All the women who had given sons to these hills and valleys only to see them raging against tyrants, shackled as slaves, impoverished, homeless, executed. What was it about this countryside and this terrible moment of history that would not allow people any loveliness or decency or peace or unity, but had to fragment relationships, rob life of all simplicity, demand terrible prices?

She was still weeping uncontrollably when she realized she

was no longer alone. He came over to her and they embraced. She still wept, but now with mingled emotions of exhaustion, confusion, joy, embarrassment, welcome. He asked her if he might bring in a couple of friends. She pleaded for a little time to collect herself.

When they came in, she did not recognize them. She had been to Capernaum a number of times and knew some people there, but not these young men. They were brothers, sons of a fishing family on the lake. He introduced them to her as Simon and his brother Andrew. Again she felt that ambivalence which drained her emotions. Personally she liked them. Symbolically they were her enemies. They were, consciously or not, taking him from her. Later on, as she listened, she realized that it was he, rather than they, who was initiating change for them all.

Over a meal he told her of his encounter with his cousin John. She could see that he was desperately anxious that she understand. He spoke of the release and self-discovery of his baptism, of becoming sure at last that he was being called to do something. He told her of the lonely days beyond the river, over on the east bank. He spoke of hunger, silence, heat, restless sleep, dreams, unrelenting thinking, deciding, struggling. She had been right. He had thought of all the possibilities she had dreaded—violence with the Zealots, solitude as a Nazarite, community with the Essenes. But he had come back now because he had chosen another way. He was going to form a community himself, a community of friends who, among themselves, in their thinking, praying, and relationships, would seek a kingdom, sometimes in retreat from, but at other times involved in, the busy world of the lakeshore towns.

They stayed the evening. Next morning when the three men left, she wept a little, but the pain was less. He had given her some money and said that more would come. She knew that her instincts had been correct. A chapter had ended. What was beginning she knew not. She felt very alone, but somehow stronger.

Nightmare in Nazareth

He came to Nazareth, where he had been brought up: and, as his custom was, he went into the synagogue on the sabbath day, and stood up for to read. And there was delivered unto him the book of the prophet Esaias. And when he had opened the book, he found the place where it was written, the Spirit of the Lord is upon me.   Luke 4:16–18

She usually received news through friends or family, and sometimes through her brother Clopas who had been in the lake towns on business. There was now, she understood, a small community who looked to her son for leadership. She gathered that he was moving rapidly around the province, preaching in the many villages and towns that dotted Galilee. Beyond that neither she nor her informants could tell what was happening. Leadership toward what? Sometimes she would find herself asking questions like that, usually feeling a vague dread of some unknown consequences.

Very brutally and without warning, her questions were answered by an incident that she would never forget. It began gently and in joy. The commotion of children in the street alerted her to his coming. She watched him from the shadowed doorway as he moved toward her. She couldn't help smiling as she saw him with the children, calling out in laughter, touching, totally at ease with him and he with them.

Later on as they sat together, he began to talk about something he called "the kingdom of God." He spoke of offering to men and women a new quality of living which was sometimes understood and sometimes not. She could see the intensity in his eyes and hear it in his voice as he said that a kind of childlikeness was necessary if people were to understand. As he spoke she could sense in him the hurt of harsh encounters about which she had heard from time to time. She tried to enter into his thoughts and feelings, to recall the bond they had known. But try as she might, she seemed to be observing this new part of his life from the outside. Ironically their very closeness was a wall between them at a time like this.

The walk to the synagogue saw their intimacy continue for a

reason that disturbed her. She was ready to take a certain grudging pride in this son who was now a name across Galilee. Yet she noticed that while they were saluted by neighbours, they were also strangely isolated. Eyes glanced; sometimes there was a smile, sometimes a murmured salutation, but there also seemed a wariness.

They separated in the synagogue. She became aware of him when the rabbi handed him the scroll. She listened as he read what everyone in the small building knew by heart, Isaiah's lovely poem—

The spirit of the Lord is upon me,
because he has annointed me.

He read it magnificently with a quiet passion. There was a pause when he had finished. She was aware of the impression he had made, aware too of the power in this man to whom she had given life. She experienced a wild hope that this might be the very moment when a door would open on all the long ago possibilities she had felt. Then he began to speak, quickly, passionately, harshly. She could feel the lash of his words on herself and on everybody there. From the first he seemed to presume their rejection of him, to anticipate and hurl it back at them. He referred to a long ago episode in the life of their ancestors, when God had spoken through the prophet Elijah to chastise and correct them. Example piled on example, each more contemptuous than the last.

By now murmurings and stirrings among the men were turning to shouts and threats. She felt herself go faint when they actually removed him from the rostrum. When she did stagger out into the street, the crowd had gone, taking him with them. She searched for support and was helped by a friend who tried to move her away. Reeling under the onslaught of all her suppressed fears, she wept uncontrollably.

Friends came later to her home to tell her that he was safe and had left the area. They mentioned nothing of the raging argument that had taken place on the edge of the rocky escarpment beyond the town. They spoke only of the extraordinary calm he had shown as his life hung in the balance, a strange and quiet authority which in the end made it possible for him to walk away from them all.

The Cost of New Wine

The third day there was a marriage in Cana of Galilee; and the mother of Jesus was there: And both Jesus was called, and his disciples, to the marriage.   John 2:1–2

She considered the invitation. The idea attracted her because such invitations came seldom. It would be a chance to meet people, some of them old friends, and to get out of the house. But she knew the real reason she would accept was that he would be there. The invitation had told her this. She reflected a little bitterly that there was probably an intended kindness behind the message. It would by now be general knowledge that she did not see him very often. Most of his life was spent down by the lake. She had heard that he was looking for lodging in Capernaum, that he was frequently seen with a growing group of followers. One of his followers was from Cana, a man named Nathaniel. Probably one of Nathaniel's friends or relations was being married.

She travelled with others who had been invited from Nazareth. She found to her astonishment that the prospect of meeting her own son made her a little nervous. Had he really become such a different person? The feeling was borne out when they met, first with their eyes across the dining room, then in the customary embrace. She found conversation difficult among the others wishing to meet him. Soon they drifted apart again, she becoming involved with old friends.

The pleasantries of the occasion continued. The young danced. After a while, with some good food and a liberal supply of wine, even the old ventured a few steps. As she sat watching and chatting, one of the family came over and whispered anxiously to her that all the wine was gone. She could sense the man's acute embarrassment as he crouched beside her, obviously trying to decide what he should do next.

Afterward she could never understand why the man came to her, nor why she suddenly knew that she should turn to her son. She was totally nonplussed by his reaction. Even now, remembering the moment, she felt its hurt. She had approached him and told him simply what she had been told. In their small town life, to have the wine run out at a wedding feast was deeply embarrassing. And she knew that he would realize this.

But his response had shocked her. The very mode of his address was harsh. "Woman" he had called her, when he all but dismissed her. She retreated from him, her eyes stinging as she held back tears. She tried to compose herself. By the time she had returned to where the family member was waiting anxiously, she had decided that it was out of her hands. She suggested that they should do whatever he told them.

What happened subsequently was now of course common knowledge in the area. It had not only solved the immediate problem at the wedding but had also made him even more a figure of fascination. As the mysterious wine had gushed and sparkled, the master of ceremonies had expressed his heartfelt relief with ecstatic compliments. She smiled at the memory of his face flushed with equal amounts of celebration and relief.

It was only afterwards, long after the feast was over and she had said goodbye to him, that she thought again of those great jars. They had been far far too much. Whatever he had done, it was unlikely to be a joke in bad taste. Her world was not one of plenty but of frugality, a society of too little rather than too much. Only when the messiah came, she had been taught, only then there would be plenty for all. The world would flow with wine, honey, milk, food, riches, peace, love.

Suddenly, as she moved around the silent house in Nazareth, she stopped, rooted to the spot. When the messiah came, she thought, there would be all the wine that could be wished for. Again there flashed in front of her eyes the picture of the six great jars. In her mind she saw his face. She thought of the voice long ago which had spoken of greatness, of things she had never really understood. The thought was blotted out by the recurring memory of his harshness. Confused, mystified, half-excited, half-fearful, she continued her work.

Time and again in her daydreaming she went back to the crowded wedding room, seeing him among the chatting, laughing throng that separated them. He appeared to her strangely powerful yet somehow vulnerable. And she remembered the words of the prophet Isaiah, words that gave her a flicker of fear.

I have trodden the winepress alone;
and of the people there was none with me.

Call to Capernaum

He had healed many . . . . And unclean spirits fell down before him . . . . He ordained twelve . . . . And the multitude cometh together again, so that they could not so much as eat bread.

Mark 3:10–20

What she could not understand was his apparent wish for confrontation. This to her seemed strange. What particularly disturbed her was his continued questioning of all that she herself, her friends, her family, and neighbours had taken for granted all their lives. She heard continually of his ability to give far more than he got in exchanges with opponents. Even people who wondered about him spoke with grudging admiration of the latest quick reply he had given to this or that well-known figure who had questioned him.

But she knew only too well that every such remark that scored a hit also created an enemy. She knew that there had been incidents in other synagogues, whole congregations shocked at something said or done. And yet everywhere there was also puzzlement. People seemed surprised, startled, but also haunted, attracted, curious. He had begun to heal. It was not an unknown gift, but he possessed it with extraordinary power and effectiveness. She was puzzled at the news that filterd up the hills to Nazareth, because on the one hand he seemed to challenge the established order—the Pharisees, the synagogue, the law—yet on the other he seemed at pains to affirm it all, to observe it, and to demand its observance in others. The more she heard, the less she understood. She prayed for him continually, not knowing what to pray for, and yet with a sense of helplessness in her love for him.

Then the letter came from Capernaum. When she read it, she realized things were worse than she had imagined. The group around him had now grown to be a tightly knit company. A whole movement was developing. It was attracting attention from as far north on the coast as Tyre. For miles beyond the lake into Idumea, from Judea, even from Jerusalem itself, individuals and groups were coming to him. The thought of Jerusalem worried her. She knew enough about the recent past to understand how carefully the powers behind those high temple walls watched the endless popular movements that began in these Galilean hills. It needed only a nod from the temple to the procurator to bring the local garrison out, and suddenly another set of crosses would stand against another skyline, and another movement would be brutally brought to an end.

The letter begged that some family members might come down to Capernaum as quickly as possible. It even expressed fear that he was being so carried away by a flood of enthusiasm that he was no longer responsible for his actions. If they wanted to avert a tragedy, something had to be done.

Her first thought was to shrink from this latest demand. She simply could not go. She would ask the help of other family members. Over the years Clopas and Mary had more and more become her resources in trouble. For them there had been family, fulfillment, mutual affection and companionship, the joy of children who, so far, seemed perfectly content to join the mainstream of life in their surrounding society. She knew it was sinful to envy, yet at times it swept over her in a flood of self-pity and resentment. Her sister-in-law Mary, the wife of Clopas, would go. With her could go one or two of their sons. If something hurtful and restraining were needed, he would receive it with least pain from those he had always known and lived with as brothers.

But when they came to make the decision, she suddenly felt impelled to go with whoever was going. She had a desperate feeling that if she did not move toward her son now, he would be gone from her forever. Even confrontation and hurt might be better than total loss of contact.

The journey took them two days. She simply had to plead for a night's rest to break it. Near noon on the second day they came over the hill to see the lake stretching away before them, blue-grey and still under a haze of heat. At the north end, its breakwater thrusting out into the lake, she could see Capernaum. As they drew near to the noise and bustle of its streets, she found herself reciting a silent prayer.

Who is my Mother?

The multitude sat about him, and they said unto him, Behold, thy mother and thy brethren without seek for thee. And he answered them, saying, Who is my mother, or my brethren? And he looked around about on them which sat about him, and said, Behold my mother and my brethren! For whosoever shall do the will of God, the same is my brother, and my sister, and mother.   Mark 3:32–35

For ordinary people the very thought of any involvement with officials from Jerusalem was forbidding. It would instinctively be felt to mean trouble. When she learned on the outskirts of Capernaum that a group from Jerusalem wished to meet the family, she felt her fears were being fulfilled. It was suggested that they meet before she tried to make contact with her son.

The interview was short, chiefly because she felt unwilling to be drawn into anything resembling a conversation or discussion. She recalled later her surprise at her own sudden calm. It seemed as if a kind of lassitude flowed through her. In the dark eyes that were focused on her, she discerned a kind of weary cynicism, a sense of *deja vu* about country prophets, amateur idealists, provincial enthusiasts. She realized with shock that these men were not in the least concerned about the substance of her son's passionate commitment, whether or not it was misguided. He existed for them only as a political question, an administrative problem requiring a decision. She realized that she was in the presence of a large and mysterious world, where affairs were manipulated with efficiency and calculation.

Then came the quiet verbal whiplash. You realize of course, the voice said, that your son is possessed by a devil? She suddenly found herself fighting for him. But, she found herself saying, I am told he drives out devils. Of course he does, came the reply as to a child slow to see a point, but he does it through Beelzebub the chief of the devils. At the last words the voice hardened.

She was not sure what followed. Her confusion arose from her fear for him, because she knew the very real threat behind the quiet accusation. She dimly heard some request being made to the men folk with her, something to the effect that they make every effort to influence their cousin before the very regrettable consequences might ensue. She found herself moving through the streets toward the house where her son was.

They had no difficulty in finding it. Even in the bustling town it was impossible to ignore the crowd. People were not only in the house but on its roof and spilling out of its door. They attempted to enter first, trying the door, then the outside stairway, but they failed. There was no obvious resentment of their effort. People seemed to be held by a voice speaking from inside the house, and they were simply not prepared to move aside to allow others in. She could hear that familiar voice. It was raised and speaking strongly. He was denying the very charge put to her about him only a short while before. "How can Satan drive out Satan?" she heard him ask. "If a kingdom is divided against itself it cannot stand." She smiled bitterly at the words. Inside herself the little kingdom of her feelings for him were so terribly divided between love and resentment, fear and hope, understanding and incomprehension, acceptance and rejection.

In the end they sent in a message to him, telling him who was outside and asking him to come out to meet them. They waited while the messenger wormed his way through the door and disappeared. For a while nothing happened. His voice went on addressing the crowd. Then she heard him pause. Immediately she began to prepare herself for the moment of their meeting. But then he spoke again across the silence. His voice was high as if raised in emotion by the occasion. "Who is my mother?" he asked the crowd. "Who are my brothers? Whoever does the will of God is my brother, my sister, my mother."

She stood reeling as if physically struck. She groped for somebody's support. She was vaguely aware of one of the men folk muttering disgustedly under his breath. Between her tears she besought them to leave, to get away from the house, from the town, above all from the voice which continued to address the listening crowd.

A Solitary Pain

When Israel was a boy I loved him; I called my son out of Egypt; but the more I called, the further they went from me;...It was I who taught Ephraim to walk, I who had taken them in my arms;...I had lifted them like a little child to my cheek, I had bent down to feed them....How can I give you up Ephraim, how surrender you, Israel? Hosea 11:1-8 (NEB)

She had dreamt again, a dream of being young. Joseph was alive. They were travelling and had lost their way. Suddenly, in the manner of dreams, they had also lost a child, then she had lost Joseph. Lost...lost...lost...dreaming and calling and crying passed into reality. And reality brought waking tears. Hurt goes deepest where love is its entry point. No loneliness is greater than where there has been ultimate intimacy. Again and again waves of self-pity swept over her, only to recede when exhaustion could take no more.

One Sabbath she found herself in a synagogue listening to a voice reading from the prophet Hosea. She recalled the tragic marriage of Hosea, his deep sense of failure and betrayal in relationships. Terrible, long-ago loneliness was in every line.

When Israel was a boy, I loved him.

Pictures flashed before her eyes. Joseph's arms lifting the child. Joseph's arms around herself. The agony and the joy of birth. The thousand things needed for a healthy child.

I called my son out of Egypt.

She remembered the first sight of Alexandria in the distance as they came out of the desert, the sea to their right, the city in front beyond the Nile. She recalled the search for work, the relief of survival. She remembered the later news that Herod was dead and that they could go back.

But the more I called, the further they went from me.

She had called in so many ways to her son, had tried so hard to follow him, to understand him, to keep up with that which called him and haunted him. And she had failed.

It was I who taught Ephraim to walk
I who had taken them in my arms.

Why was it that when relationships went sour, one preferred to forget the agony of adult disagreement and return to the simpler years of dependency?

Suddenly there was the sword again, the sword of old Simeon. It was never far from her thoughts.

The sword shall be swung over her blood spattered altars.

Again the old and never distant fears gripped her. Yet the ambivalence remained. It seemed to defy her to lose faith with the past, to refuse to allow her to forget a voice and a face now almost never seen or heard.

In the synagogue it was quiet and cool and shadowed. Only yesterday James had come to her to tell her of a recent meeting between Jesus and himself, and his other brothers and sisters. It had been difficult. He, James, had tried to bridge the distance. There was no dislike. It was merely the great distance between childhood associations and the understanding of adult years. Someone among them was affecting the lives of thousands of people in their immediate world, attracting and inspiring, speaking of new worlds of the spirit. Yet those who accepted him as an orphaned brother, felt strangely toward him. They found it exasperating to find words for what they felt. James, who felt drawn to Jesus, could only help because he himself was at times puzzled.

She understood James' puzzlement only too well. He had told her about the family's decision to go to Jerusalem for the feast, and how they had encouraged Jesus to go if he wanted to contact as many people as possible. James had then asked her if she wished to come with them. She had thought about it. For a moment a long-forgotten excitement shot through her, an image of the city as she and Joseph had first seen it. Just as quickly a memory of cold, threatening eyes pierced her, the eyes of the official from Jerusalem, eyes of establishment, power, and authority.

She thanked the family for the invitation. She preferred to leave Jerusalem as something held in her memory. For some reason she could not have put into words, the actuality of visiting it again repelled and frightened her.

The Dark Night

Have mercy upon me, O Lord, for I am weak; O Lord, heal me, for my bones are vexed. My soul also is sore troubled:...I am weary of my groaning; every night wash I my bed, and water my couch with tears. My beauty is gone for very trouble, and worn away because of all mine enemies. Psalm 6:2–7

Where she had grown up, people tended to avoid public prominence. To become highly visible in a volatile society where many struggled constantly for power, was to court danger. Again, the atmosphere of the time, especially in this little country, was fought with a mingled anxiety and euphoria. The times were hungry for change and liberation. Messiahs were sought and therefore tended to appear. Usually they were ignored until their movement petered out, or if it grew to significant size, they were quickly and savagely eliminated by the authorities.

From the beginning she had always feared for her son. There had been the first ecstatic days when the future seemed boundless and she felt like a queen of countless possibilities. That confidence and anticipation had been first shaken by the words of old Simeon. Later they had been traumatically damaged by the massacre that her family had only barely survived. There had been many days of quiet joy and remembered loveliness, but somehow she had learned to expect such periods to end in shattering experiences fulfilling her fears and sapping her ability to affirm the future.

Like great dark monuments these events measured her life. The encounter in the temple when he was twelve. The realization in Cana that she no longer knew this intense and powerful stranger. The lash of his rejection in Capernaum. Her increasing inability to understand the dream that for so many others seemed more and more to be inspiring and captivating.

Sometimes in moments of particular weariness or loneliness, she realized that there was an even greater demon with which she had to struggle, the question of faith itself. She could never banish from her mind the terror and ecstasy of the long ago moment of proclamation. All her life she had never doubted the reality of that experience. In terrible moments it had been the rock to which she had clung, the light in her darkness. That she had been called from beyond her own imagination and desires she was totally certain. But the hideous demon of doubt towered above her when she contrasted the early hopes with the subsequent course of events. At such times she questioned not so much the fact of the encounter but the purpose of it. What was it all for?

Somebody had come to her and told her of the desperate message Elizabeth's imprisoned son John had sent from the hellish dungeons of the fortress of Machaerus on the Dead Sea. "Art thou he that should come," John had asked, "or do we look for another." She thought of how often she had wanted to scream out her doubts in that kind of question. Her mind reeled at the thought of facing the man she had carried in her womb and pleading with him to end her doubt, to answer the unnumbered questions, to give order to the inner chaos from which for her there seemed no escape. For others he was what they were beginning to call the Way. She had heard that expression. She had reacted bitterly because of the utter contrast to her own experience. Sometimes she wondered if her own inner agony was the sword that had been predicted, and when she thought of this there came a wild hope that it was so. So she tried to transfer to herself the danger and suffering that she foresaw and feared more and more for her son.

It was some months now since James and Mary and the others had gone to Jerusalem. She had gathered that there had been a public scene more than once, and at least once a dangerous brawl. It had confirmed her fears. Since then Jesus had not come north again. The last she had heard was that he and the young men from Capernaum were hiding somewhere north-east of the city. Not long ago the flowering branches of scarlet bougainvillia reminded her that in a couple of weeks it would be Passover. Very soon the procurator's guard would be moving from Caesarea on the coast to Jerusalm, to the residence and barracks in the Antonine tower near the temple. The pulse of the city would quicken. The political temperature would rise. She wondered where he was at this moment in northern Judea. She prayed that he and the others would remain there.

The Coming of the Sword

Then Jesus six days before the Passover came to Bethany, where Lazarus was which had been dead, whom he raised from the dead....Much people...knew that he was there: and they came not for Jesus' sake only, but also that they might see Lazarus also, whom he had raised from the dead. But the chief priests consulted that they might put Lazarus also to death; Because that by reason of him many of the Jews went away, and believed on Jesus. John 12:1–11

She knew immediately that there was bad news. It was written in every line of her sister-in-law's face. In the next hour or so Mary, Clopas' wife, shared with her all the news that had come from their son James, who had been in the Jerusalem vicinity.

After the exhausting week of confrontation in Jerusalem, Jesus and the others, as she had known, had left the city. It had been her fervent prayer that they would stay away at least until things quietened. And so they had. They had crossed the river and vanished into the desert wilderness area beyond. It was the area from which John the baptizer had emerged, blazing with a prophetic and fatal passion. She couldn't help wondering if there was any significance in the fact that her son had returned after all the years to where his cousin had chosen a way other than love and care and gentleness, rather a way of condemnation and judgment. Would Jesus now emerge, reflecting images of the messiah for which some friends had searched in vain?

When her sister-in-law told her why he had come out of hiding she could scarcely believe it. A year or so ago there had been an episode in Nain not far from Nazareth. It had involved the funeral of a young man. Apparently her son had revived him, and the countryside had been agog. She had known also about his friends in Bethany, south of Jerusalem, and he had often spoken of Lazarus. Mary related to her the events as they had happened. Now the consequences had to be dealt with. The news of it had spread all over the south, and of course, into Jerusalem. After all, Bethany was only a stone's throw away. From James' report, the event had once again thrown wide open the public debate about Jesus. And it was being carried on at every level, from the bazaars to the Sanhedrin itself.

Meanwhile, up to the time when James' messenger had left for Nazareth, no one knew what Jesus was going to do next. James' fear arose from the fact that all Jesus' actions seemed to be more and more public. Once again the country was preparing for Passover, with its excitement and crowds and the ever present danger of some flash-point. Already there had been a great many visits to the house in Bethany by officials from the city. There was also a rumour that the Sanhedrin was eyeing not only Jesus but also Lazarus for arrest.

Mary Clopas ended the grim recital, her eyes watching her sister-in-law very closely. She noticed the cost of the last few years etched into her face. It was an aged face, not by length of years but by depth of what had had to be borne. She herself yearned to communicate the hope she had in this situation, the hope that now at last people would listen, would be drawn by the wonder of what Jesus had done, until they would be captivated at a much deeper level by the person himself, as she had been, and James, her son. She found herself fiercely willing this disappointed and confused woman in front of her to see the possiblities, to get in touch with the tremendous reality her own flesh and blood had created. She left to the last James' invitation. He had suggested that his mother return bringing her sister-in-law with her. He had done this because he felt certain that things were moving to some kind of climax. He could not be certain to what kind of resolution things would move. They could be on the verge of a breakthrough in Jesus' dealings with the society around him. Jesus could also be in terrible danger. So James had suggested they come.

A few days later she was climbing the remembered hill road from Jericho. It had been about eighteen years since she had come this way. Joseph had been beside her, and there had been a boy of whom they were extremely proud. This time she came as a middle-aged woman seeking again the person she had once sought as a child in the temple, not knowing this time who or what she would find. Beside and around her, trying to be of help, were her sister-in-law and others. Some of them she knew, and others she did not wish to know. Among them walked yet another Mary, a follower of her son from the lakeside town of Magdala.

The Hill

Now there stood by the cross of Jesus his mother, and his mother's sister, Mary the wife of Cleophas, and Mary Magdalene.   John 19:25

She noticed that the young Roman guard who came by curtly asking them to keep back was little more than a boy. He and the other members of the cohort in charge of the executions realized their own vulnerability in these moments. Around them there usually milled a crowd of spectators, including very often individuals crazed with grief. If the prisoners were political, there was always the danger of a rescue attempt, especially in the early stages of the crucifixion process.

She had rested, if it could be called that, in the house at Bethany. She had arrived too late to meet him before he had left for the last time, the day before Sabbath. She had listened with horror to the way in which he had thrown himself against the city, first in the procession to the gate and subsequently in the direct attack on the temple trading area. All that last day she had heard the visitors come and go in the house, but she knew she was being allowed to rest only because there was no good news to tell her. Very late at night they wakened her to say that he had been taken. Finally she had been introduced to a young man from Capernaum whom she remembered from that painful visit over a year before. He could hardly control himself as he told her the news of the impending execution. To her surprise she found herself comforting him. In some way she could not understand, she knew she had arrived at this moment with long preparation. When he asked her what she wished to do, she said calmly that she wished to go to the place.

Their destination was visible long before they reached it. In a sense this fact helped her to prepare herself. As she walked the last few hundred yards towards the area, the crosses slowly grew. The figures gradually formed. Nevertheless when she was close, close enough to see features, she was thankful for the arm supporting her. At first a wild hope grasped her that it was not her son at all. The body was revealed in total and terrible degradation and defilement. She realized that it was no worse than what had been perpetrated on others all around her. Like others she had avoided close acquaintance with the obscenity of crucifixion.

As the young Roman guard passed, she shuffled back with John who stood supporting her. She looked upward across the filthy ground between them and the crosses. It occurred to her that all her life she had been distanced from him. Even at his presentation she had looked across a barrier in the temple while the priest took her child further beyond her reach before returning him. Almost always it was across barriers and walls and chasms that their relationship had been conducted and their elusive love communicated. Yet always both on his part and on hers there had been love. Of that she was certain. Even if they had not succeeded in naming its presence, it was always there.

Someone had told them how long it had been since the execution began. It now looked as if the end could not be far off. By now the front of the crowd had inched forward again. She was aware with a sense of mingled terror and joy that he had opened his eyes and had seen them. She could see his lips moving, trying to form some word. Careless now of any restraint she moved forward to try to catch the sound.

When the whispered croaking sank to silence and the eyes had closed again, she had already moved back and begun to lean even more heavily on the young arm of John. This friend of her son's, unknown to her until a short time ago, had now become her son by the whispered statement from the dying man above them. This evidence of his concern for her, even in his extreme agony, was for her a mingling of pain and appreciation. He had addressed her even now in that distant way of all the adult years. For him she was "woman," though she consoled herself that indeed he had also used the lovely and loving word mother when his eyes had moved from her to John.

With the help of other friends, some familiar and others unkown to her, John persuaded her to move away. She never heard the terrible cry of desolation that took all but his last breath. But the sword which later pierced his side was no sharper than the sword she had known through all the years leading to this day.

85

Sleeping and Waking

The ransomed of the Lord shall return, and come to Zion with songs and everlasting joy upon their heads: they shall obtain joy and gladness, and sorrow and sighing shall flee away.

Isaiah 35:10

When she lay awake, as she often did, she would see him. In those hours of sleeplessness his face would change according to the rhythm of her remembering. It would be that of a baby sucking at her breast, or of a tiny child taking his first stumbling steps in the lodging in Alexandria. Sometimes it would be the shining eyes and endless energy of his days in Nazareth. On and on the faces paraded in her mind. Now and again there would flash between them the ghastly mask she had looked up to on that last day, and just as quickly it too would disappear, some other memory quickly superimposed on an agony too difficult to dwell upon.

She was aware, of course, of the experiencs reported around her. Weeks ago in Nazareth John had told her with shining eyes and excited voice of the events within hours of her last terrible glimpse outside the city. She bitterly regretted not having gone to the tomb with her sister-in-law and the girl from Magdala. Whatever they had seen or heard had elated them beyond belief, yet, not having been with them, she felt only greater confusion and emotional exhaustion.

They had had to leave the rooms in Jerusalem and come home again. Even those who were totally convinced that the impossible had happened were not sure what course of action to pursue. As well, there were in Nazareth and Capernaum anxious families who had been left behind. So one day they had set out, and she went with them, hardly aware of the hazards and strain of the journey, barely conscious of heat and cold, moving in and out of conversations dimly overheard as if from a great distance.

That had been weeks ago. By now she was beginning to feel a little more familiar with the sights and sounds of Capernaum. Sometimes at night she would wake from dreams of the home in Nazareth only to hear the sound of the lake water lapping on the nearby shore. The realization that she might never again find home in Nazareth gave her mingled regret and relief. At this particular time every single experience seemed to bring with it a welter of conflicting emotions that usually left her totally drained. She could see in people's eyes that they still worried about her, still waited for her to regain her energy and interest in life. But it seemed to her that she had lost too much. There was nothing left. The sword had pierced something vital.

When they came to her with the news of their decision to return yet again to Jerusalem, she rebelled. All the pain and resentment of his involvement, of the movement, of these strangers from half of Galilee and beyond who had robbed her of so much of him, all came out in a flood of anger that left her exhausted. As always it was Clopas' family who understood and helped. James, the nephew who seemed daily more mature and understanding, allowed the flood of her anger and tears and self-pity to wash over him until it had abated. Then patiently and lovingly he explained why they were going. He spoke of the experiences some had had. He told her of the morning fog lifting on the lakeshore, of the voice, of the meal, of the absolute certainty of the reality of it all. He told her of their growing conviction that they were being directed for some reason to Jerusalem. Beyond this they knew nothing, only that the eternal city called them, or a power and a will was urging them to return.

Later, when she thought about that time together in Capernaum in John's house, she wondered if James' voice had been alone in her mind, if James' eyes alone had looked into hers, if James' hand alone had touched her. After they had talked, she had slept, and in her sleep the faces had come again. But this time the fearful mask was gone, and in its place was the face she remembered from the afternoon they spent together before the incident in the synagogue in Nazareth. From that day she had begun to recover, to feel energy return. The terrible weight seemed to lift from her body and her mind and her heart, releasing her from an emotional and spiritual tomb

When they left for Jerusalem, she was among them. One night as they rested, she recalled the time they had turned back to the city to find a boy, so many years before. This time, she thought, she was once again in search of him.

The Breaking of Bread

These all continued with one accord in prayer and supplica-
tion, with the women, and Mary the mother of Jesus, and with
his brethren. Acts 1:14

Sometimes she felt amazement when she looked at some of
the people around her, especially the men. They came from
one of the hardiest livelihoods in existence, subject to all the
insecurities of seasonal weather, highly competitive, often
dangerous. Lake fishing for a living did not encourage the
gentler virtues. Yet here they were, haunted and held by
something they had encountered on that lakeshore and had
sacrificed endless time over, during the last few years. The
extraordinary thing was that now there seemed to be no end to
it. They had become a community, and she herself had survived and been given strength by the immense affection shown
to her.

She found herself thinking of all this again as she watched
the piece of home-made bread pass from hand to hand toward
her. She had got used to this moment now. They did it
whenever they were together, any small gathering of his
followers. They were not all here in this house; others had
gone to find shelter either with friends or relations or at an inn.
Some had gone into Jerusalem hoping to stay with various
families. In the Bethany house she had been welcomed by
those whose friendship had meant so much to her son. John
and a few others had stayed here.

The bread came near to her. Suddenly it was in John's hand,
and he was hesitating before turning to her. She had not so far
been able to take part in this simple but terrible action. Even in
symbolism her whole being rebelled against this eating and
drinking of the body and blood of him who was of her own
body and blood. Again she felt conflicting feelings sweeping
over her, taking away her ability to think and act. She realized
that every eye around the table was on her. She became aware
of the circle of faces. Once they had been strange and often
resented because of the close friendship they had had with
him, the kind of friendship she had longed for so desperately.
But now she saw them differently. She realized the love and

support this circle, and even a greater circle not with them at the moment, had given her. The depth of all this love entered into her. It seemed to her swimming eyes that all their faces became one, and she knew that the single face was his, and that the love in their faces and the love in his face was one and the same love. She found herself eating and drinking, the rough bread melding with her body and the wine stinging its way into the centre of her being.

Suddenly she was aware of absolute silence, and she knew she was with him again. She could never be sure later if any words were spoken. She often tried to capture his appearance, as indeed they all did, but she found it impossible. She and they could only say that it was him, yet more intensely and more vividly him than at any moment of encounter she had ever known. And then he was gone, and in some way they were released. Yet they felt released for a purpose.

As if by silent command they moved from the house and out beyond the village. When they came to an open area and found others newly come from Jerusalem, they neither felt nor expressed surprise. They were conscious only of sharing an expectation. The silence was total, as if this hillside had been isolated from the surrounding world and time. In the silence he came among them and in touching one another they were aware of touching him and he them. Suddenly they knew that this hour was both an ending and a beginning, both meeting and farewell. Overcome with emotion some cried out as if questioning. But their voices died away into silence. Some stood holding up their arms looking into the darkening sky. Then a few suggested that they return to the city and get some rest. Others began to sing softly.

They came down the hill, some back to the house, others turning west toward the city. As they did so, they were conscious of being many yet somehow, in a way beyond words, they felt themselves to be one. Among them she walked, supported by John and by her sister-in-law Mary. On every side of her, in the touch of their hands, in the sound of their voices, in the forms moving about her in the lightening dawn, she was aware of a Presence. As she looked, the sun breasted the Mount of Olives and flooded the city with the glory of a new day.

The Roadway to the Stars

While Mary disappears from us as a woman of flesh and blood, living somewhere through the eventful first years of those growing communities, which would one day in far away Antioch be called Christian, she remains in the forefront of Christian history. Whatever be our particular stance toward a concept such as her bodily assumption into the heavenly realm, an unarguable fact remains: in the consciousness of Christians, Mary never died. For the twenty centuries of our history we have remembered her in innumerable ways. This awareness has existed on many levels, from thankful recollection of her role in the divine drama as described in the New Testament, to claims of her power so extravagant that more than once in history a responsible voice has had to counsel carefulness, and to call a retreat from ultimate claims about her.

The history of Christian thinking about Mary is full of the most appalling misuses of scriptural allusion, side by side with concepts that help us to see her role, and God's ways, vividly and unforgettably. After only a very few centuries, Mary is seen as a second Eve knitting up the ravages of Eve's action in Eden, and as Noah's ark carrying the new life and a new future. She is seen as a bush burning with life, and again as the ark of a new covenant, carrying Christ in her womb as Israel's ark carried the tables of the law.

In the late fourth century, adoration of Mary is thought to bring military salvation to the threatened eastern empire. In this Byzantine civilization she becomes the conqueror of (and replacement for?) the countless forms of the feminine face of divinity shown in Cybele, Diana, Isis, Minerva, Juno, Aphrodite. When the navies of Byzantium sail down the Aegean from Constantinople, their great sails bear her image, as would the ships of Spain centuries later.

Ambrose in Milan speaks of Mary as herself the church, in that she is the mother of all Christians. Later on Augustine in North Africa teaches that she is sinless. In the Nile valley especially she becomes a rich symbol for Coptic Christianity. When women's orders began to form in Europe, she is chosen as patroness.

For millions of ordinary men and women in every century, she would become intercessor, the feminine figure in a masculine Christian pantheon of Father and Son. Her voice in vision would be experienced often, sometimes creating vast shrines where millions would flock. Among these places are Lourdes in France, Walshingham in England, and Knock in Ireland.

It is sometimes suggested that the church managed all this for various exploitive purposes. There may well have been instances of such things, but if the role of Mary in the Christian centuries is regarded with any degree of openness, the seeker will discover something quite extraordinary. Far from her presence being a product of church encouragement or manipulation, it is true that in Mary the Christian church has repeatedly found itself faced with a phenomenon that continues to pulsate through time, almost in spite of the church! We begin to realize that the legend of the angels bearing Mary's tired and worn body to her Creator is a human attempt to express something impossible to explain yet equally impossible to deny. This "something" is the fact that, at least in some sense, Mary does not die, and that she has proved in countless lives to be a channel for the grace of her son.

We have come a long way from the simplicities of Nazareth and the wife of the carpenter. We began our journey in the reality of those fields and houses and human lives. Now let us see where the flesh and blood journey may possibly have ended.

We watch her return to the city with the small community of men and women who had experienced the mystery we call the Ascension. And we see two roads of possibility stretching into the future. One is short and leads us only as far as the valley of the Kidron, a mile or two away. The other stretches far to the north-east, and takes us to the vast cosmopolitan city of Ephesus on the Aegean coast of Asia Minor. In speaking of these two roads, we of course refer to differing traditions that have come down to us.

The tradition that Mary came to, and subsequently died in, Ephesus, begins with her being given by her dying son into the care of his friend John. This fact, noted in St John's gospel, is linked to the fact that since the first century, a strong connection has existed betwen John and the area around Ephesus. However, the early traditions of John in Ephesus do not link the mother of Jesus with him in this region. Not until about the eighth century do we find the tradition that, following the very early persecutions of the community in Jerusalem (mentioned in the Acts of the Apostles, chapters 11 and 12), John, with many other Christians, left the city and took Mary to Anatolia.

By far the earlier and stronger tradition sends us down the shorter road from where we stand near Bethany. We can walk in a very short time to the deep, sun-drenched valley below the east wall of today's Jerusalem. As we do so, we may take a moment to reconsider the links in the long chain of memory binding us to the remote past of these ravines and brown hills. It may help us to realize that the links are not as tenuous as we might suppose, and that today is not as hopelessly separated from our most sacred yesterdays as we might think.

The great links that bind us to those very early Christian years could have been forced by accidents of history. However, we may also see them as providential rather than accidental.

The first link is forged from the fact that, almost from the very beginning, the Christian communities in Judea and Galilee possessed a strong sense of place. Where they felt some event of significance had occurred, they often marked the spot in a way that indicated its significance.

Over two centuries went by and the world of the empire changed. The emperor himself became Christian. Under a new regime there came a passionate (and often domineering and cruel) determination to do honour to the places of Christianity's birth. All over the holy land the remembered places of earlier generations were visited, and wherever there existed an already ancient shrine, usually primitive and often crumbling, the art and engineering of the Byzantine empire were applied, and a basilica soon stood above the spot.

The tide of history changed again. In the seventh century there emerged from the deserts another army. It followed a new vision of God both beautiful and terrible. Its name was Islam. Significantly for us Islam accorded to Jesus of Nazareth and his virgin mother great honour. For that reason Islam tended to spare those places connected with Mary's memory, among them, incidentally, the Church of the Nativity which stands today in Bethlehem.

We move from the seventh century to the eleventh to hear the sound of other armies clattering through ancient places. Armed with the power and money of medieval Europe, Crusaders sought out the Byzantine sites and above them erected their own great stern churches, whose soaring walls and carved entrances anticipated the richer Gothic world that would one day beautify Europe.

To such a place and among such walls we now walk, to make our final rendezvous with the woman whose life we have tried to touch.

We are passing where the road to Jericho crosses the Kidron valley. The upper church, built long ago by the Byzantines, has gone. In its place are the remains of the Crusader shrine. We move down steps which are long and wide. They begin in the blazing sun and deposit us in candlelit gloom, deep in the earth. Around us in this earth lies the dust of Crusader queens. A little further down we stand in the older walls of Byzantium, and then approach the tomb itself. Around it the Crusaders placed a band of script.

This is the Vale of Jeosaphat,
where begins the roadway to the stars.
Mary, favoured of God, was buried here,
and incorruptible was raised to the skies.
Hope of captives,
their path, their light, their mother.

As we stand here, it should not shame us but rather give us all joy, that as we claim her son to be our brother, his life and death to be our Way, so we may claim this woman to be in God's providence and choosing "our path, our light, our mother."